SECURITY

FOR LIBRARIES

PEOPLE,
BUILDINGS,
COLLECTIONS

Edited by

MARVINE BRAND

AMERICAN LIBRARY ASSOCIATION

Chicago 1984

Designed by Vladimir Reichl

Composed by FM Typesetting Company
  in Linotype Times Roman and Helvetica

Printed on 55-pound Glatfelter,
  a pH-neutral stock, and bound
  in 10-point Carolina cover stock
  by Cushing-Malloy, Inc.

Library of Congress Cataloging in Publication Data
Main entry under title:

Security for libraries.

  Bibliography: p.
  Includes index.
    1. Libraries—Security measures. I. Brand, Marvine.
Z679.6.S4   1984   025.8'2   84-455
ISBN 0-8389-0409-2

CONTENTS

PREFACE

Until recently, libraries in educational institutions paid little attention to security. But today, violence and disasters occur, collections dwindle, and attendant legal problems persist, so that library administrators must keep a watchful eye on their building(s) and equipment; their collections, records, and computer data; and their employees and users.

At the same time, library people are turning to each other and to interested organizations for suggestions and support in dealing with security. That is why this volume, which was proposed by the Books and Pamphlets staff of the American Library Association, focuses on new information on security for libraries. Though the discussions center on university, public, and school libraries, the volume can be of value to librarians in other institutions.

In the introductory article, Thomas Shaughnessy recommends that every library establish a security plan, provide written procedures for implementing it, and conduct in-service training. In the second article, Wilbur Crimmin gives sensible advice and procedures for institutional, personal, collection, and building security concerns in libraries.

In the third article, Janelle Paris examines the situation faced by almost all libraries: whether to rely on in-house security protection or to seek assistance from outside the library. Barbara Bintliff and Al Coco, in the fourth article, alert the reader to the duties owed by the library to its users to provide a secure and safe place for both their persons and belongings. They also discuss some of the legal consequences in carrying out security measures and procedures by describing the most typical security problems in libraries and civil liability.

Walter Wicker's concluding section, on selected readings on security, provides a timely bibliography on a subject that will demand more of our attention in the future, and more of our budget dollars.

These articles and accompanying information will not answer a multitude of new questions that will challenge libraries in the years ahead. But of all questions that come to mind, perhaps the most haunting has to do with tolerance: Has our tolerance for crime and negligence increased to the extent that our libraries are in jeopardy?

In the final analysis, libraries have to cope with security in an individualistic but lawful way—some applying drastic measures and others applying only minimal but constant measures. But in this uncertain world, *anything* can happen, and usually does, even in libraries.

MARVINE BRAND

ACKNOWLEDGMENTS

Warm words of appreciation go to John J. Miniter, Professor, School of Library Science, Texas Woman's University, Denton; Edward G. Holley, Dean, School of Library and Information Science, University of North Carolina, Chapel Hill; Stephen R. Salmon, President of Carlyle Systems, Berkeley, California; Charles Churchwell, Director of Libraries, Washington University, St. Louis, Missouri; Charles Griffen, Business Technology Library, Hartford Public Library, Hartford, Connecticut; to the authors of the articles; to Herbert Bloom, Senior Editor, American Library Association; and to my husband, Johnnie L. Brand. I am grateful for their contributions.

THOMAS W.
SHAUGHNESSY

SECURITY: PAST, PRESENT, AND FUTURE

The last several years have seen a dramatic increase in the problems encountered by libraries in maintaining the security of their collections. To the extent that the literature of a field is a valid index of its concerns or preoccupations, there was a 385 percent increase in the number of articles dealing with the topic in the 1960s over the 1950s, and a 156 percent increase in the 1970s.

Articles on Library Security in *Library Literature,* 1950-1979

	Articles Indexed	*Percent Increase*
1950–1959	27	—
1960–1969	131	385
1970–1979	336	156

It is also interesting to note that "vandalism" became a subject heading in *Library Literature* in 1964, and in 1970 the heading "library protection systems" was introduced.

To a certain extent, these figures parallel nationwide increases in crime statistics, as well as the growth of expenditures for various forms of security services. The problems of shoplifting, pilferage, petty theft, and similar crimes have grown to alarming proportions.[1] And more serious crimes are also on the increase. Nationally, reported cases of robbery rose

---

1. R. S. Post and A. A. Kingsbury, *Security Administration* (2d ed.; Springfield, Ill.: Charles Thomas, 1973), p. 3.

from 60 per 100,000 population in 1960 to 191 cases in 1978. Cases of larceny or theft rose from 1,035 per 100,000 population in 1960 to 2,744 in 1978.[2]

In response to these trends, it is estimated that American firms will spend $21 billion on security by 1990, compared with $5.8 billion in 1978—an increase of 12 percent per year.[3] Within this picture, expenditures for electronic alarm systems will increase by over 15 percent annually.[4]

One might be tempted to assume that certain institutions, such as libraries, would be immune from criminal acts and the attendant problems of social disorder. But it must be remembered that libraries developed in response to certain sociocultural circumstances, and it is in their interest to adjust to the turbulent environment in which they exist. The problem of theft has plagued librarians for centuries, but there is particular cause for concern today because of the sharp increase in losses during the past decade.[5]

The problem today is not simply preventing the theft of resources, or even attempting to diminish the loss rate. The whole question of library security is a much larger, more complex matter. The emphasis continues to be on the physical safeguarding of materials; however, the concept must be extended to include the security of data and files, as well as the personal safety of employees and library users. Security may be operationally defined as providing the means, active and passive, which serve to protect and preserve an environment which allows for the conduct of activities within the organization without disruption.[6]

Although security encompasses major disasters such as fire, flood, earthquake, etc., these areas will not be treated in this paper. Instead, it will focus on preventing individual acts which inhibit or prevent library users and staff from locating all the materials owned by the library, from safely using or working in the library, and from maintaining security of certain files and records.

2. U.S. Department of Commerce, Bureau of the Census, *Social Indicators III* (Washington, D.C.: Government Printing Office, 1980).

3. "Security Equipment Purchases—1978–1990," *National Petroleum News* 72:33 (July 1980).

4. Ibid.

5. Philip P. Mason, "Archival Security: New Solutions to an Old Problem," *American Archivist* 38:477 (Oct. 1975).

6. Post and Kingsbury, *Security Administration*, p. 5.

The Literature
on Library Security

The history of security in libraries is interesting. Most articles on the subject, as well as the actions taken by libraries, focus on the theft of books and other library materials. As one writer suggested, the purpose of the medieval practice of chaining books to tables was their safekeeping; therefore, it constitutes an early security measure.[7]

Most early works on the subject reported on the results of inventories. Although security *per se* was not addressed in the literature until the 1930s, these articles discussed missing and misplaced books.[8] However, there appeared to be reluctance on the part of librarians to consider the possibility that some of their misplaced stock might well have been stolen. This reluctance seems to have continued among archivists even to the present time. According to Philip Mason, the reluctance, and in some cases outright refusal, of archivists to admit publicly that they have been victims of theft is perplexing.[9] Many archivists are unaware of widespread evidence of theft and believe that their experience is unique.[10]

The 1940s saw the publication of Thompson's important work on bibliokleptomania.[11] But once again the theft of library materials was presented as an abberation, and the focus of the article was on the perpetrator, rather than on preventive measures which libraries might consider. The problem of library security was viewed as unidimensional: books were sometimes misshelved (and therefore lost), and occasionally they were stolen. When it was reported that library materials had been mutilated, the mutilation did not consist of pages ripped from books and journals, but primarily margin jottings, underlining sentences or words in library books, and similar acts of defacement.

In the 1950s, the literature on library security, curiously, was sparser than in the preceding decade. Despite the decline, however, librarians and archivists seemed to be gradually awakening to the gravity of the security problem. In a 1956 article, Robert H. Land addressed the theft of papers

7. Carol W. Tyler, "Book Theft: A Brief Review," *Cornell University Libraries Bulletin* 202:9 (Oct. 1976).

8. "Library Security: An Overview," *Library & Archival Security* 4:7–8 (nos. 1/2, 1982).

9. Mason, "Archival Security," p. 478.

10. Ibid.

11. Lawrence S. Thompson, "Notes on Bibliokleptomania," *New York Public Library Bulletin* 48:723–60 (Sept. 1944).

and manuscripts by both scholars and employees.[12] He suggested that the most effective solution was to prosecute offenders as vigorously as possible.[13] The implication was that if prospective thieves were aware of the penalties, they would not attempt to steal. However, two years later, in 1958, a person posing as a scholar stole—with considerable ease—a number of valuable documents (letters signed by Jefferson and Franklin) from the New York Public Library.[14] Then, when the documents were returned to the library, the thief, in spite of Mr. Land's earlier injunction, received a suspended sentence.[15]

In view of the social unrest of the 1960s, it is not surprising that there was an enormous increase in the number of articles on library security during this decade, a trend which continued into the 1970s. The landmark survey of library progress, *Libraries at Large: Tradition, Innovation, and the National Interest,* published in 1969, revealed that among college, school, and public librarians "the most-often-expressed trouble and worry on a day-to-day basis related to students' manifest disrespect for public property and the theft and mutilation of books and other library material."[16] It was during this period that major acts of vandalism were committed against libraries: card catalogs were damaged, library buildings burglarized, and some fires were set, in addition to mounting evidence of theft and mutilation of library materials. As a result, the concept of library security had to be broadened to accommodate a variety of criminal acts, even though the main focus continued to be on theft and mutilation. The intrinsic trust of librarians for their publics was gradually but markedly eroding.[17]

Fortunately, the acts of physical violence perpetrated against some libraries in the 1960s did not mark the start of a trend. However, these events served to awaken archivists and librarians to the extreme vulnerability of collections, and the very inadequate (and sometimes nonexistent) security measures available in many libraries and archives. The size of many archival collections, often in the tens of thousands of pieces, precludes item-by-item identification.[18] There is even a question as to whether a library or archive should stamp its ownership mark on a par-

---

12. Robert H. Land, "Defense of Archives against Human Foes," *American Archivist* 19:121–38 (April 1956).
13. Ibid.
14. "Thieves," *Library & Archival Security* 4:17–18 (nos. 1/2, 1982).
15. Ibid., p. 18.
16. D. M. Knight and E. S. Nourse, *Libraries at Large: Tradition, Innovation and the National Interest* (New York: Bowker, 1969), p. 114.
17. "Library Security: An Overview," p. 9.
18. Mason, "Archival Security," p. 478.

ticularly valuable or fragile document because of the damage this might cause to the item.[19]

Apart from potential damage to collections, the events of the decade underscored the need to protect valuable records, such as the card catalog and shelf list. A number of libraries proceeded to microfilm both sets of records in the late 1960s. But as more and more libraries convert their bibliographic records to machine-readable form, other security measures will be required.

The literature on library security during the decade of the 1970s was characterized by reports on the effectiveness of various electronic theft-detection systems, by reports of major losses on the part of libraries and archives, and by studies of the motivation and psychology of those who steal or mutilate library materials. But perhaps the most significant development in the literature on this topic occurred in 1975 with the appearance of the *Library Security Newsletter,* which in 1980 became the *Library and Archival Security* journal.

As was indicated earlier, a number of libraries have made the case that electronic security systems have been effective in reducing theft. There is also evidence, however, that these gains may be counterbalanced by the significant increase in the crime rate, in terms of both violent and nonviolent acts, such as theft, and by the increasing sophistication of thieves. With regard to the former trend, the General Services Administration reported an increase of 122 percent in incidents of all types in government-owned buildings in just a one-year period![20] An example of the second phenomenon is the report (in *Library Journal*) of the use of fraudulent borrower cards in a number of public libraries[21] and the theft of art work from two libraries in New England.[22]

Academic libraries were not exempt from the problem either. A report of the Carnegie Council on Policy Studies in Higher Education, published in 1979, noted as one of the signs of deterioration of academic life the "theft and destruction by students of valuable property, most specifically library books and journals."[23] It states, furthermore, that the theft and

19. "Marking of Materials," *Library & Archival Security* 4:48–49 (nos. 1/2, 1982).

20. *Annual Summary of Incidents Occurring in Buildings Controlled by the General Services Administration, 1978* (Washington, D.C.: General Services Administration, 1979), p. 4.

21. "Library Security: Book Thefts Are Up," *Library Journal* 100:352 (15 Feb. 1975).

22. "Art Works Stolen from Two New England Libraries," *Library Journal* 100:1592 (15 Sept. 1975).

23. Carnegie Council on Policy Studies in Higher Education, *Fair Practices in Higher Education* (San Francisco: Jossey-Bass, 1979), p. 3.

mutilation of library materials is a problem on most campuses.[24] And *Change* magazine claimed in 1977 that the theft of manuscripts and documents had reached alarming proportions.[25]

In direct reaction to these conditions, the Society of American Archivists established a registry of stolen materials in 1977, and over 2,000 missing items were immediately reported. In 1979 the Antiquarian Booksellers' Association of America approved guidelines for dealing with the problem of theft.[26] The association will also make space available (at modest rates) in the *A B Bookman's Weekly* to list or describe materials which have been stolen from libraries and archives.

The 1970s also saw the publication of studies and articles on the characteristics of persons who steal or mutilate library materials. Thompson's article on bibliokleptomania,[27] which he published in 1944 and updated in 1975,[28] had served for at least two decades as the seminal work on the subject.

In a study[29] conducted at Kent State University, 168 students were interviewed concerning their knowledge of and participation in the mutilation of periodicals. Fourteen students (8.3 percent) admitted to mutilating journals, but a number of students appeared to be unconcerned about the matter. More importantly, statistical tests revealed few differences between mutilators and nonmutilators, although the former group held generally less favorable opinions about the library. It appears that acts of mutilation depend more upon immediate situational circumstances (for example, the library was about to close or the copy machine was out of order) than a premeditated plan to mutilate.[30]

A similar study was reported on in 1981.[31] Out of a sample of 201 undergraduates, 84 percent reported that they never took books without checking them out, or removed pages. Those who *did* commit acts of theft or mutilation were found to be good students who did not expect to be caught. The author suggests that up to 8 percent of the student body may

24. Ibid., p. 11.

25. "To Catch a Thief," *Change* 9:19 (Feb. 1977).

26. "Theft Guidelines Now A.B.A.A. Policy," *A B Bookman's Weekly* 64:2252–54 (8 Oct. 1979).

27. Thompson, "Notes," p. 727.

28. Lawrence S. Thompson, "New Reflections on Bibliokleptomania," *Library Security Newsletter* 1:8–9 (Jan. 1975).

29. C. Hendrick and M. E. Murfin, "Project Library Ripoff: A Study of Periodical Mutilation in a University Library," *College & Research Libraries* 35:402–11 (Nov. 1974).

30. Ibid., p. 408–9.

31. Dana Weiss, "Book Theft and Book Mutilation in a Large Urban University Library," *College & Research Libraries* 42:341–47 (July 1981).

"actively steal books."[32] The students' attitudes toward the library and the availability of photocopy machines were found to be unrelated to theft and mutilation. Some students tend to place preparation for a professional career above the observance of library rules and policies. The author also believes that academicians seem to tolerate theft and mutilation because of student efforts to maintain their grade-point averages.[33] Similar observations have been made by Guy Lyle in his book *The Administration of the College Library*.[34]

Although these works focus on security problems in the academic library, all types of libraries seem to be affected. Many school librarians list theft as a major problem.[35] According to one librarian, libraries find not only books missing but lamp sockets empty, ashtrays missing from smoking areas, and washrooms bereft of towels, despite daily restocking.[36]

A review of literature published between 1980 and 1983 shows no evidence of any lessening in the trends described thus far. Extremely rare materials were stolen from Harvard's Museum of Comparative Zoology[37] and from the Peabody Institute Library.[38] Five libraries in the Pacific Northwest have reported that their entire twenty-volume sets of *New Grove's Dictionary of Music* have been stolen.[39] On the positive side, the arrest and prosecution of James Shinn, who has been involved in an extraordinary number of thefts from libraries, represent a major step toward dealing with such criminals.[40]

Electronic Security Systems

One of the most significant advances in library security occurred in the latter part of the 1960s with the development of electronic theft-detection systems. A number of academic and public libraries quickly installed such

32. Ibid., p. 344.

33. Ibid., p. 346–47.

34. Guy R. Lyle, *The Administration of the College Library* (4th ed.; New York: H. W. Wilson, 1974), p. 77.

35. J. W. Griffith, "Library Thefts: A Problem That Won't Go Away," *American Libraries* 9:224 (April 1978).

36. Ibid., p. 225.

37. "Harvard Zoology Library Counts Rare Books Lost," *Library Journal* 106:1874 (1 Oct. 1981).

38. "Security Problems in Libraries Mount," *Library Journal* 106:1873 (1 Oct. 1981).

39. "Security in Libraries," *Library Journal* 107:586 (15 March 1982).

40. "Security Problems in Libraries Mount," p. 1873.

systems, and in 1970 the American Library Association published a *Survey of Theft Detection Systems.*[41] All of these systems operate on essentially the same basis. Specially treated tags are placed in library materials and as these materials are taken past sensing screens, they trigger an alarm.[42]

Most electronic security system manufacturers offer their systems in two versions. The "full circulating" system permits the library to desensitize the electronic tag in each item which is borrowed. Thus a person who has borrowed books earlier in the day may carry them in and out of the library during later visits. This version is particularly popular in academic and school libraries; however, it costs more and requires that library materials be "resensitized" as borrowers return them to the library.

The "bypass" system does not offer the capability of desensitizing tags. As materials are charged out, they are passed around the sensing screens and thereby bypass the security system. Although these versions are less costly, they are suitable mainly in libraries where borrowers do not make repeated visits with previously charged-out materials.

A number of studies have indicated that electronic security systems have been successful in reducing theft. It has been reported that many of these systems have virtually paid for themselves (in terms of reducing losses) within three years.[43] It was estimated that by 1979, approximately 6,500 libraries worldwide had installed such systems.[44]

Although security systems have been successful in preventing casual theft and in detecting actual attempts at theft, all such systems may be circumvented by a determined or knowledgeable thief. With some systems, the electronic tags are fairly obvious and may be peeled off or cut from the pages or covers to which they are attached. Furthermore, tags in some full-circulating systems may be desensitized with small but powerful magnets, and aluminum foil has been used to shield books with tags from registering on sensing screens at library exits. Also, books may not register on some systems if they are carried through the sensing screens at a certain angle.

An important related consideration is the percentage of a library's collection which is actually tagged. When electronic security systems are installed in libraries, certain valuable or high-risk collections are tagged

41. "Survey of Theft Detection Systems," *Library Technology Reports* (Chicago: American Library Association, 1970).

42. Alice H. Bahr, *Book Theft and Library Security Systems, 1978–79* (White Plains, N.Y.: Knowledge Industry Publications, 1978), p. 34.

43. Nancy H. Knight, "Security Systems," in *The ALA Yearbook, 1980* (Chicago: American Library Association, 1980), p. 280.

44. Ibid.

first, followed by new materials as they are acquired by the library. For example, reference books, bound journals, reserve materials, and art books would typically be tagged first. Other categories might also be identified, depending on the library and its clientele. The remainder of the collection might be tagged "on the fly"; that is, as books are returned from circulation, sensitized tags would be placed in them. Because of the time required to tag a large proportion of the collections, libraries which suspend the practice of checking briefcases and bags at too early a date are obviously placing their collections in jeopardy.

There are at least three other potential problems associated with these systems. The first of these concerns the possible damage to library materials caused by the adhesives used on the tags and the high acidity of the paper used for some sensitized labels.[45] Secondly, there is a question whether these systems may cause health problems. Many of them emit low levels of electromagnetic radiation, which are well within U.S. safety standards, but they exceed the standards of some European countries. As a result, some of the systems are not marketable in those countries.[46] A related question concerns what effect, if any, these devices have on heart pacemakers. It has been reported that such systems interfere slightly with a particular type of pacemaker, but overall they do not present a significant hazard.[47] Thirdly, there is some evidence to indicate that those systems which operate on an electromagnetic principle are not always compatible with automated circulation systems which are located in proximity to them. Signals emitted by the security system may interfere with the operation of the circulation system.[48]

Despite these problems, there is no doubt that these devices have significantly contributed to reducing the theft of library materials.

Other Types of Security Systems

Prior to the invention of electronic security systems, libraries used, and continue to use, a variety of methods for maintaining security. These include closed stacks, library guards and patrols, posted penalties for theft and mutilation of materials, and tagging, marking, or property stamping— to name just a few.

45. Ibid.
46. Bahr, *Book Theft,* p. 35.
47. Knight, "Security Systems," in *ALA Yearbook, 1977,* p. 299.
48. Bahr, *Book Theft,* p. 35.

Closed Stacks. In terms of collection security, the closed stack seemed to be the prescription for several decades. In practice, however, truly closed stacks rarely existed. In academic libraries, for example, faculty members, and often their teaching and research assistants, had access to the stacks, and toward the end of the closed-stack era, graduate students and honors program undergraduates frequently had access. There seems to be no doubt, however, that collections maintained in closed stacks are more secure than those on open shelves, even though they do not address the problem of internal theft. Also, there is less opportunity for a book to be misshelved (and thereby lost to prospective users) in a closed-stack library.

Closed-stack or restricted-access collections of today are typically comprised of rare books, archives, and other special collections. The importance of maintaining the security of such collections, most will agree, far outweighs the need of users to be able to browse through them.

Guards and Patrols. Few surveys have been done on the use of guards in libraries. One, in the late 1960s, indicated that guarded turnstiles were used by 80 percent of the libraries which had any type of security system.[49] However no study has attempted to evaluate the effectiveness of guards in terms of maintaining the security of collections and the feeling of safety on the part of library users and staff. It seems that most libraries (and museums, galleries, etc.) use them as a deterrent to book theft and other crime. And many law enforcement officers stress that crime prevention is equally important as the arrest and prosecution of offenders.

Among libraries which use guards, there is a large variation in how they are used. Typically, guards are identified by their uniforms, but in some libraries, regular staff members and even student assistants perform this function without an identifying uniform. Also, in some situations, uniformed guards are used chiefly to patrol the library and regular library staff serve as turnstile checkers, whereas in other situations the reverse is true. There is also variation in how much checking is done upon users' leaving the library. Typically, handbags or purses are not checked nor are bulky coats, be they worn or carried. For the most part, bags, briefcases, and (on college campuses) the ubiquitous backpack are the only accessories checked.

Not only is there wide variation in how guards are used in libraries, differences also occur with respect to the supervision of guards. On some campuses, for example, all uniformed officers are members of the university police force and, consequently, are on the police force's budget. In

49. Ernest E. Weyhrauch and Mary Thurman, "Turnstiles, Checkers, and Library Security," *Southeastern Librarian* 18:112 (Summer 1968).

public libraries, an "outside" contract security agency might provide guard service. And in other situations, guards may be on the library's payroll. Obviously, the range of services rendered to a library by its guards is determined by the control the library has over them.

According to Alice Bahr, one of the chief disadvantages of library guards is their cost.[50] In an attempt to lower their security costs, some academic libraries have contracted with their university police departments for "community service officers" or "cadets." These are employees of the police department who have been screened and given police and first-aid training. They are not armed, as police often are, but often wear an identifying shirt or belt and carry two-way radios for contact with the police. In some instances, students are hired for these positions. In libraries, they may be assigned at turnstiles or make regular patrols of the library building.

Tagging Library Property and Equipment. As many libraries have evolved into learning resources centers, their security concerns have correspondingly broadened to include the costly equipment and software which now characterize them. Some libraries which do not collect films, audio or video cassettes, phono discs, slide-tape programs, etc., have become involved with data bases and computers and therefore need to be concerned with the security of very valuable equipment.

There are various methods for securing such equipment, but none, unfortunately, is foolproof. One approach is to attach small metal property tags to all equipment. While such tags are very difficult to remove, they may be defaced without much difficulty. A variation of this method is to etch the name of the library or parent institution directly onto the equipment, sometimes in a concealed location. It is believed that if stolen property is recovered, this system will enable the rightful owner to identify and claim it.

Another approach is to identify equipment which is easily movable or transportable with eye-catching painted stripes or with the institution's logo, spray-painted on the equipment. Equipment which is not designed to be moved (for example, typewriters, turntables, and computer terminals) should be bolted down. If conditions warrant, metal covers are available which fit over such equipment and permit the use of the equipment, but not its removal or disassemblage.

No matter what approach is taken, it is imperative that every library maintain an up-to-date equipment inventory. The inventory should include an item-by-item listing of each piece of equipment, with its serial number and purchase price. For equipment which is transportable (such

50. Bahr, *Book Theft*, p. 87.

as film and slide projectors, calculators, etc.), a highly secure storage room or cabinet is a necessity. This storage facility might be used to house the original or master copies of audiovisual programs as well.

Security of Cash. Apart from the inherent value of library materials and equipment, the cash that is typically found in libraries can be a particularly attractive target for theft. Many libraries have vending machines (of one type or another) that are sometimes located in staff lounges, but also in areas that are open to the public. Photocopy machines, which are coin operated, and dollar-bill changers are other attractive targets. Often, photocopiers and vending machines are not owned by the libraries which have them, but are placed in libraries on a contract basis. Nevertheless, the fact that these machines are available in most libraries raises important security questions.

In addressing these issues, library administrators must insist that all coin-operated machines and bill changers be made as secure as possible. Coin boxes should be strengthened with steel bands and enclosures, and wall-mounted dollar-bill changers should be very securely attached to the wall. Most important, however, is insistence on the part of the library that all coin boxes be regularly emptied, even on weekends (if the use of such machines warrants it).

The location of coin-operated machines within a library also has implications for their security. Although, from a user point of view, it may be convenient to disperse photocopy machines throughout the library building, their dispersion in remote locations often invites theft.

Finally, the number of keys to vending machines and photocopiers should be kept to an absolute minimum. If the machines are not owned by the library, it would be appropriate that the library not have access to them at all. If coin-operated photocopiers, typewriters, terminals, and bill changers are owned by the library, a regular and frequent schedule of emptying coin and bill boxes must be followed, with the funds from each location recorded separately and deposited each day. On weekends, all collected coin and cash should be placed either in a night depository or in the library's safe (filing cabinets, desk drawers, and other "hiding places" are not acceptable).

And just as keys to the coin boxes should be highly restricted, so should the combination to the library's safe. The safe should be in an interior office which has a security lock on its door, and if conditions warrant, the safe may be connected to the local police department by a silent alarm system. Safes are also useful in libraries which collect fine money. In some instances, a good deal of cash may accumulate, and whenever this occurs, it should either be placed in a safe or deposited.

Additional Considerations. The design of a library building has much to do with the degree of security that may be normally maintained in the library. Obviously, libraries with multiple entrances are more difficult and costly to secure than those with fewer exits. Adequate surveillance is likewise more difficult in buildings which offer numerous isolated areas, or where lighting is below standard. Such areas may be used for mutilating library materials.

In older library buildings, windows may present a problem. Books have been dropped from open windows to avoid checking them out. Emergency exits, where alarms are not connected to a central control panel, may also be used to remove materials from libraries. Some emergency exits are equipped with simple, battery-powered "local" alarms which may sound only when the emergency door is opened. The result is that such alarms may not be as loud as necessary, and they sound for too short a time. Without connection to a central control panel, staff members who hear the alarm may be hard pressed to pinpoint its location quickly.

For buildings which, because of their design, are very difficult to secure, closed-circuit television cameras might be appropriate. These devices are particularly useful for observing remote or problem areas, such as loading docks and passageways. Of course, staff are required to tend the television monitors, and this considerably increases the cost of this approach.

Just as alarms and closed-circuit television serve as deterrents to crime or the improper use of library facilities, some libraries post signs which indicate the penalties for theft and defacement of library property. Again, however, there is no evidence of the effectiveness of this approach. Indeed, the use of such signs may be questionable in view of Weiss's study which indicates that college students who steal books do not expect to be caught.[51] Signs may be useful and appropriate in that they indicate that libraries take the security of their collections seriously, and this is certainly a step in the right direction.

Security of
Information and Records

Although the literature on library security has focused on the theft and mutilation of materials (physical security), two other types of security will, in all probability, need to be thoroughly addressed in the future. The first of these is information security. Traditionally, libraries have main-

---

51. Weiss, "Book Theft," p. 344.

tained confidentiality with respect to borrower files and loan records. In-formation concerning the borrowing patterns or information requests of individuals has not generally been divulged. Observance of the library user's right to privacy is a significant responsibility of all library staff, and is specifically addressed in the American Library Association's "State-ment on Professional Ethics" (1981).

It may be that security with regard to these records was not a major concern in the past, simply because of the difficulty in retrieving infor-mation on library usage from systems (manual files, photographic records, or key sort systems) which, until fairly recently, were widely used. Some assessments of such systems indicate that they are barely able to provide currently valid data on overdue loans, much less information on the usage habits of specific individuals or groups.

Computer-based circulation systems have dramatically changed this situation, however. Borrowing records can be easily and rapidly retrieved, along with patron information. And although special "passwords" are typically required to enter various files, the security of many computer systems is regularly breached. Students on some campuses have devised ways to change course grades stored in a computer, and many cases have been reported of transfers of funds from one account to another by unlaw-ful use of computers.

Libraries that have public-access terminals which are part of integrated systems (catalog, acquisitions, and circulation functions) are particularly vulnerable to problems of information security. One solution to these problems is to delimit the functions which may be performed on certain terminals. For example, public-access terminals to an on-line catalog should permit only the retrieval of bibliographic information on library holdings, while terminals designated for the use of technical services staff permit retrieval, input, and editing functions. Terminals in the circulation department should be limited to recording loan transactions, maintaining borrower records, and performing operations related to this function. These "terminal permissions," by which certain functions may be per-formed only at designated terminals, are controlled by computer software. Even those who have valid passwords or codes cannot perform functions (such as data entry) at terminals which are not designated for the purpose.

Passwords are another means of controlling access to information stored on computer tapes or discs. The use of passwords will prevent un-authorized use of a terminal which may be restricted to certain functions (for example, bibliographic data entry). One password may be used for certain operations, or each staff member who is authorized to perform certain operations may have a unique password. To maintain financial accountability, it may be desirable for circulation department staff to have individual passwords which must be used to record payment of library fines.

The security of data in computer files can be strengthened by the use of duplicate back-up discs or tapes, which should be stored in a location separate from the original data records. In the event of unauthorized tampering with library records, or a disaster such as flood or fire, the library would not lose records that might be irreplaceable. If such a loss *did* occur, the most that would be lost would be the acquisitions, cataloging, circulation transactions, and patron records for one day.

Similarly, a duplicate copy of the software which drives a library's automated system should also be kept on hand, in a separate location. Should someone very skilled in computer technology be able to bypass various security screens and gain access to the software itself, it is possible that computer programs could be modified so as to prevent their proper functioning. Should this occur, the duplicate software could be utilized, thereby minimizing downtime and inconvenience to library users and staff.

To summarize, information in computer-based library files is made secure, first, by a system of "terminal permissions," by which software permits only certain operations or functions at designated terminals; second, by means of "passwords" which enable a terminal operator to perform certain functions at that terminal; and third, by producing, on a daily basis, backup records of all library files, including catalog data, circulation transactions, etc., which are stored in a separate location.

For records which are not in a machine-readable format, some libraries have produced microfilm copies. In the event of fire or other disasters, a microfilmed copy of a library's shelf list would significantly decrease the damage resulting from loss of an original shelf list or card catalog. Again, it is essential that this backup copy be stored in a secure area, apart from the library building.

Personnel Records. Typically, other types of information are stored in libraries which require special security measures. Probably the most prominent are personnel and employment records. Although library administrative officers (library director, assistant directors, and personnel officer) normally have free access to such files, care must be taken that authority in this sensitive area be not broadly distributed. And while the "Open Records Act" grants employees the right to examine the contents of their respective personnel records, they should not have access to other records in the same cabinet or file drawer. Also, records to which the employee has waived his or her right to examine (such as letters of reference) should be removed from the file by an administrative officer before it is given to the employee.

Although personnel files are typically stored in locked filing cabinets, which are located in fairly secure offices or rooms, certain additional security precautions are called for. With regard to employee access to their own files, it is recommended that such access be "by appointment only" and that it occur in the presence of a personnel officer or other responsible individual. It is also suggested that the employee sign in on a log and indicate the date and time of day on which he or she examined the file. There should be space on the log for the initials of the library official who supervised the file examination.

By requiring an appointment to examine personnel files, the library administration has an opportunity to remove material, temporarily, to which the employee has waived his or her right of access. And by requiring that the examination be conducted in the presence of a library official, unauthorized removal of any information is prevented. The employee's signature on a file-access log is simply one more safeguard to ensure the confidentiality of personnel records.

Present Trends and Future Directions

Against the backdrop of increasing theft of library materials, on the one hand, and the rapidly rising costs associated with the replacement of stolen materials and equipment on the other, one may conclude that library security will receive considerably more attention in the future than it has in the past. Every library manager will have to become much more concerned and informed about the matter, and the security-consciousness of all library staff members will have to be raised. Although there is the view that too much emphasis on security might conflict with the goals of service to users and open access to information,[52] librarians also have the responsibility of being accountable for the materials left in their care. It is not sufficient, moreover, to assume that installation of an electronic theft-detection system will solve all security problems. What is needed is formulation, in each library, of a security plan, written procedures for implementing it, and in-service training for library staff on how to deal with security problems.

The plan should be comprehensive and address in detail the following broad areas: (1) library collections in all formats, (2) library equipment (office, audiovisual, vehicles, etc.), (3) bibliographic records (regardless

52. "Theft Detection and Prevention in Academic Libraries," *Spec Flyer,* no. 37 (Oct. 1977).

of format), (4) personnel records, (5) security of employees, (6) security of library users, and (7) building access and key policy. Other areas may also need to be included, depending on the situations. For example, the library's parking lot may need to be incorporated in the plan if there have been incidents where automobiles, belonging to patrons and/or staff, have been burglarized or vandalized.

Library Collections. With regard to library collections, all types of library resources need to be encompassed: books, journals, microforms, computer software, manuscripts, maps, audiovisuals, art works, and realia. As was noted earlier, electronic theft-detection tags are often more easily attached to books and journals than to other forms of information. Consequently, different approaches may be necessary to protect audiovisual, microform, map, and manuscript collections. In some instances, restricted access or use may be required; in others, well-trained security guards or closed-circuit television surveillance may be appropriate.

It is also important to protect library materials throughout the acquisitions process. Obviously, newly acquired titles which have not been marked with a property stamp are very susceptible to theft. Similarly, gift books, which have been received but not yet sorted and screened, need to be protected. Gifts may be particularly vulnerable because staff may consider their removal an unofficial "fringe benefit," rather than theft.

To prevent the theft of newly received materials by library employees or custodians, library managers must devise strategies which accommodate both the protection of these materials and their accessibility to staff for processing. In other words, *inventory control* must be applied from the moment of receipt of material—and not, as so often happens, only when the item is placed on the shelf for use.

Although employee theft of materials is a sensitive topic, it can frequently be addressed by in-service training programs. The staff member who takes a newly received and unaccessioned book or journal home may simply not be aware of the problems this can create for the library.

Inventory control of library materials includes a number of important related issues. Among these are procedures for the withdrawal and disposal of materials no longer needed by the library. In some jurisdictions, library books are regarded as public property and therefore must be disposed of in the same manner as other types of surplus property (such as vehicles, equipment, and furniture). In other situations, library materials may simply be withdrawn and then discarded or sold.

Secondly, inventory control is based on the assumption that management knows what is in the inventory. Or, to put the matter differently, is it logical to assume that one can control an inventory if inventory records are not periodically checked? It is true that small and medium-size libraries *do* conduct periodic inventories, but this practice is not followed in large, research-oriented libraries because of the costs of conducting them. But an inventory of all monograph collections, completed at the University of Houston Library in 1982,[53] illustrates that it is possible to inventory a research library collection in a relatively short period of time, without exorbitant cost. It seems likely that more and more libraries will conduct periodic inventories in the future, not only to get a grasp on losses but also to improve the success of users in accessing needed materials.

Library Equipment. The library security plan should address all types of library equipment and furnishings, including vehicles. Once again, an inventory of all equipment and furniture is a prerequisite for their control. Whenever feasible, movable equipment should be bolted to work surfaces. But even this does not eliminate the need for identifying, by etching or marking in some fashion, each item in the inventory. Identifying marks on equipment and furniture should not be placed in obvious locations. Thieves will often attempt to remove such marks before they attempt to dispose of stolen property.

All portable equipment should be stored in locked cabinets or storage rooms. The security plan should specify those staff members who have keys or access to this equipment. It is also important to take note of equipment components which are easily removed, for example, lenses to microform readers, diamond styluses, headphones, slide carousels, etc. Staff should be trained to be vigilant with respect to the security of such items.

As libraries increase their acquisition of nonprint media and a steadily expanding range of services is provided (for example, computer-assisted instruction and services to the handicapped), there will be increasing dependence on special types of equipment. Consequently, great emphasis should be given to this matter in every library's security plan.

Bibliographic Records. Just as the library's key policy specifies which staff members shall have which keys, the security of bibliographic software and records requires a similar policy with respect to passwords. The policy or plan should also specify the safeguards for protecting bibliographic records. Many libraries have a record of their shelf lists on microfilm, while others maintain duplicate or backup copies of circulation records and catalog data on computer tapes and discs which are housed in a separate location.

53. Thomas W. Shaughnessy, "Procedures for Inventorying and Replacing Missing Monographs in a Large Research Library" (unpublished report, University of Houston, 1982).

It is possible that the need for these safeguards will decrease in the future, as more and more libraries convert their records into machine-readable form. The data might then be stored in a bibliographic utility to which the library belongs, or at some other node in a bibliographic network.

Personnel Records. Perhaps in the future there will be less concern over the security of personnel records for the simple reason that very few individuals would put anything in writing which might, however remotely, result in litigation. Most library administrators will confirm that letters of reference have become almost useless in employee evaluations or in the recruitment process. Frequently, they are testimonials to good character, and say little or nothing about performance. A similar phenomenon may occur with respect to internal evaluations of staff. Despite these conditions, staff members are entitled to have their personnel records protected from unauthorized examination. For this reason, the security policy should address this matter and protect the records of unsuccessful applicants for positions as well.

Safety of Employees. Among the quality-of-worklife issues that have emerged in recent years is employee safety. Employees, except those who hold hazardous jobs, normally expect to work in safety and with some feeling of physical security. The library's security plan should address this matter, and include procedures for securing the personal effects and vehicles of library staff. Ideally, with regard to personal belongings, staff members should be provided with a locker or lockable desk in which to leave their effects. The objective is to prevent the theft of personal belongings by other staff members and by persons from outside the library. Employee vehicles may need to be protected by fencing or extensive illumination of the parking lot, or by means of a guard who is stationed there.

In large libraries, it might be appropriate for all staff to wear an identifying badge. This would be useful in preventing unauthorized access to areas which are not open to the public. The security policy should also address the location of work stations and the times during which such stations are staffed. For example, staff members should not work at isolated work stations, or when there are few, if any, other employees around. A related issue is provision of escorts for staff who work at night, to assist them in reaching their cars or public transportation. This service is already provided at a number of academic libraries.

In terms of staff productivity and morale, staff members who pilfer and steal are a far greater threat than strangers. To preclude the hiring of employees who are dishonest, library personnel officers will have to do a much more thorough screening of applications. Also, the library needs to establish training programs to motivate employees to avoid losses (whenever possible) and to take precautions in securing their personal belongings, as well as those of their colleagues.

Safety of Library Users. Just as library staff should be able to expect a safe environment in which to work, library users should be able to expect safe surroundings. To the extent that intellectual freedom is based upon free and uninhibited access to library resources, libraries have the responsibility of creating and maintaining atmospheres in which such access can occur.

This is a difficult topic for the library administrator to address because personal safety is often a matter of individual perception. Library users may feel safer in some libraries than in others, or less safe on a particular floor of a library than on another floor. Frequently, the time of day influences these perceptions.

Clearly, library managers cannot deal with the entire range of user perceptions, but they can take steps to reduce patron anxiety and insecurity. First, all parts of the library building, including restrooms, stair wells, and stack areas, should be adequately illuminated. Large buildings which are well illuminated appear to be far more hospitable than those which are not. Second, it is helpful if uniformed guards or easily identifiable library staff members make periodic tours of the building. Third, it might be appropriate to locate telephones throughout the stack areas. These phones need not be equipped with dials, and can be linked either to a service desk or guard stations. The mere removal of one of these phones from its receptacle should enable a guard to pinpoint its location in the library and render assistance (if necessary).

Finally, it is important that a certain level of discipline be maintained in libraries. Too much noise or socializing among library users can give the impression that library staff are not in control of the facility, and this can create feelings of unease and insecurity among library users. In some libraries, this is such a significant problem that extraordinary measures may be required—for example, requiring identification for admittance or employing armed guards.

Building Access and Key Distribution. Systems for controlling and auditing locks and keys are of major importance in any loss-prevention and security program. No lock is more secure than its combination or the keys that operate it.[54]

The library's security plan should minimize the number of master and building-entrance keys that are given out. Staff who have keys should

54. Charles F. Hemphill Jr., *Management's Role in Loss Prevention* (Chicago: American Management Association, 1980), p. 167.

understand that they are responsible for maintaining possession of their keys at all times. Keys should never be lent because they can be quickly and easily duplicated.

Records should be kept of all keys issued to employees. If an employee is terminated or assigned to new duties, library managers should either collect the keys, prior to releasing the employee's final pay, or review whether the employee will continue to need specific keys.

All keys should be identified by code or number, and should not indicate the doors or locks they will open. Keys which are not assigned to individuals on a regular basis should be stored in a highly secure key cabinet. Of course, access to this cabinet should be highly restricted.

The library security plan might also determine which staff members may have access to the building when it is closed. Janitors and custodians typically require such access, and this may also be true of certain staff members.

It is appropriate for the plan to specify the procedures by which the building is secured at the close of operations. Care must be taken that all users have left the building before it is closed and that all exterior doors have been secured.

Conclusion

For the library administrator, it seems very likely that security will occupy an even greater amount of staff time, will consume a larger portion of the library's budget, and will heighten the tension between the library's responsibility to make resources accessible, on the one hand, and to protect and be accountable for them on the other. However, concern for security must be broadened to include far more than resources, and it is for this reason that libraries should establish a comprehensive security policy.

Undoubtedly, new technologies will be developed to assist libraries in strengthening their security, but for the short range, provision of security will continue to be a labor-intensive operation. With regard to resources stolen from libraries, it should be possible, in the not too distant future, to list these items in a central data base so that they can be accessed on-line. Printouts of stolen materials could then be photocopied and rapidly made available to local book dealers. This system would not replace the listings service of the ABAA, but complement it.

Finally, many libraries, particularly those in urban areas, must address the sensitive question of the use of library facilities for purposes which are not directly related to library objectives. Although the poor, the unemployed, and the homeless have used libraries as places to escape from cold and rain, there is a question as to the effect that extensive loitering has on the perceptions of users who seek library materials or information. Obviously, this is a very difficult and sensitive issue, which may need to be addressed on the basis of local circumstances. In worst-case situations, as in many others which are discussed in this chapter, regular in-service training programs for staff will be the key to the library's success or failure. In the last analysis, a dedicated, security-conscious staff contributes significantly to any security program.[55]

Checklist for a Security Survey

When a library staff becomes security conscious, an almost infinite list of security issues or concerns can be developed. The topics which are cited below are only some of the factors which should be part of any library's security survey. The list is by no means comprehensive and is illustrative of only some of the more important security matters.

1. Security of Collections in All Formats and Equipment
   a. Electronic security systems
   b. Closed/restricted collection-access policy
   c. Guards, exit attendants
   d. Publicizing penalties for theft and mutilation
   e. Property stamping, equipment tagging
   f. Current equipment inventory
   g. Equipment storage lockers
   h. Vehicle security and access policy
   i. Proper identification of users or borrowers
   j. After-use procedures to determine damage (if any)
2. Security of Cash
   a. Vending machines: food, photocopier, etc.
   b. Change machines
   c. Access to coin boxes, cash registers
   d. Access to library safe
   e. Cash-handling procedures and accountability
3. Bibliographic and Patron Records
   a. Terminal access, permissions
   b. Passwords

55. Bahr, *Book Theft*, p. 112.

    c. Backup tapes/discs/software

    d. Policy on off-site locations of backup data

    e. Microfilm duplicate records

4. Personnel Records

    a. Access policy

    b. Supervision of record examination

    c. Use of logs to record access

    d. Policy on removal of confidential documents or other data

    e. Secure storage

5. Employee/Patron Security

    a. Exit/entrance controls

    b. Use of emergency exists

    c. Building design/surveillance

    d. Patrols or TV monitors

    e. Building-access policy

    f. Staff ID badges

    g. Emergency telephones

6. Key Policy and Building Security

    a. Procedures for issuing and reclaiming keys

    b. Periodic lock changes

    c. Silent alarms

    d. Parking lot security

    e. Adequate lighting

    f. Custodial services access

    g. Window and book-drop security

7. Other considerations

    a. Liability and other types of insurance

    b. Legal counsel provisions

    c. Access to library lawyer for periodic meetings

    d. Budget implications for security measures

*WILBUR B.
CRIMMIN*

INSTITUTIONAL, PERSONAL, COLLECTION, AND BUILDING SECURITY CONCERNS

The focus of the discussion that follows is on the medium-size library—on the assumption that smaller libraries can scale down from what is offered and that the giants will already have scaled up. Secondly, the focus is on the public library, although the issues affect academic and school libraries as well. Academic, school, and special libraries will find their security needs addressed as a part (only) of overall corporate, school, or academic security strategy; so their areas of responsibility and choice tend to be somewhat restricted. Some notes, toward the end of this article, briefly describe the relationships of these libraries to the security arrangements of parent institutions.

Why Security?

Why *not* security—when the alternatives are low staff morale, missing equipment, diminishing collections, vandalism, and (in the worst-case scenario) loss of the "whole store"? If supermarkets estimated shoplifting losses at more than $1 billion in 1981, can supermarkets of books— that is, libraries—be considered exempt from loss? If the U.S. Department of Commerce estimates that burglary, theft, and vandalism cost industry $3 billion annually, can library administrators afford to be complacent? The answer to both questions is, of course, *no*.

What Is Security?

The definition that will be used as a working thesis is this: security exists in situations where harm and loss can be controlled within certain acceptable minimums *and,* moreover, where those involved in the situations perceive them to be controlled.

Perfect security never did exist, and never will, in this chancy world. But controls which enhance security *do* exist, and it is the library administrator's responsibility to be aware of and to employ those that are most suited to his or her (usually unique) situation.

Controls range from hardware to electronics to memoranda. The task is to pick and choose, weighing cost and gain. Administrators usually find themselves climbing toward higher levels of security a step at a time. Rarely will they find themselves in a situation where all elements of an integrated security program can be implemented at once. (Even in those situations, searching reappraisals of the system should be scheduled.)

Is There Such a Thing as Too Much Security?

Of course, there is the possibility of "too much" security, because twentieth-century capabilities have substantially outrun normal library needs. It is a rare library indeed that will require, or can afford, voice-imprint or hand-geometry identification systems.

As has been found with so much of modern technology, the fact that something *can* be done does not mean that it *should* be done. The library administrator who confuses his or her institution with NORAD is making an expensive mistake. On the other hand, the administrator who ignores security is making an even greater mistake.

An administrator who has decided to conduct a security survey is cautioned to keep five elements in mind: the library as institution, the site, the building, the collection, and the people (staff and public) who use the first four. There are two reasons for caution. First, administrators will find that whatever action they may take to secure one of these elements will almost invariably impact on one or more of the others. Second, keeping all five elements in mind will protect them from mistaking a partial solution for a total solution.

For example, these five elements will protect them from neglecting an evacuation plan because a fine fire detection system has been installed, or from assuming that an electronic detection system adequately protects a collection that readily can be passed, piecemeal, through unscreened windows.

The Library as Institution

Insurance. In their personal lives, individuals often think of security in terms of insurance; and insurance is no less important to the library as institution. As an institution, the library needs and should have fire, valuable papers, and liability insurance, with as many riders to policies as appropriate or required.

The employee of the library should be covered for (or should seek) medical insurance, life insurance, workers' compensation insurance, and unemployment insurance. If the library is also a city department or part of a university or school system, these insurances may be provided by the parent administration, either as self-insurer or in combination policies.

However, two types of insurance are often ignored, but should be considered by the security-minded administrator. The first is *bonding.* Bonding protects the institution from the depredation of those who, by authority granted, have access (in particular) to the funds of the library. Bonding is inexpensive, and it is, after all, twelve long months from one audit to the next.

The second type of often-ignored insurance is *association liability* or *errors and omissions* insurance. Policies of this type will protect the institution, the trustees, and the administration in the event civil suits are brought that charge malfeasance, errors, or omissions in the exercise of official duties. The fact that trustees usually serve without wage or profit will not necessarily protect them from such suits. The administrator owes it to the trustees to see that they have this degree of security.

Rules and Regulations. In one sense, many procedures of the library are designed to provide security for the collection. However, this section concerns rules and regulations that affect security of persons, furniture, and equipment.

It is hard for staff or public to feel secure in an institution whose standards of behavior must be guessed at or that vary from department to department. Trustees owe it to staff and public to develop, adopt, and post rules and regulations. (There is, after all, a world of difference between directing offending individuals to posted rules and regulations and the alternative of being obliged to tell them that you find their behavior objectionable!)

Rules and regulations are invariably stated (as were other, more famous commandments) in the negative: "Thou shalt not . . ." They may include such language as the following:

1. Smoking, eating, and drinking are forbidden.
2. Disruptive noise or behavior and abusive or profane language are forbidden.
3. Behavior that endangers oneself or others is forbidden.
4. Actions that result in damage to library buildings, furniture, equipment, or material are forbidden.

Each board of trustees will want to develop language appropriate to its library's situation, and it is usually well to "file a disclaimer"—that the posting of specific rules "does not permit, license, or condone any act forbidden under federal law, the statutes of the state, or the ordinances of the city."

In any case, it is important not only that trustees adopt and post rules and regulations but also that, in doing so, they make manifest by whose authority behavior in the library is governed. Trustees will often find that such authority has been delegated to them to "adopt such reasonable rules and regulations as may render the use of the library and reading room of the greatest benefit." A corollary authority is sometimes appended: "to exclude those who willfully violate such rules."

Authority to Act in Emergencies. The security of a library is imperfect unless the staff knows, and the public can find out, who has the authority to act. In colloquial form, "Who is in charge here, anyway?" The staff has a need to know and the public has a right to know.

If the top administrator is "in residence," the answer should be evident. However, life and the library go on in the administrator's absence. Evenings, Saturdays, and meetings will frequently find him or her elsewhere. The answer to the question "Who is in charge?" should be equally evident at those times. The solution is simple: issuance of a memorandum listing those authorized to act for the library in an emergency, with an addendum giving order of precedence. It thereupon becomes a simple clerical routine to see that all service desks have weekly lists of those in charge. (This is important information, whether an emergency occurs or does not.)

In preparing the addendum it is well to keep in mind that precedence should be given to those stationed nearest the location where an emergency might occur. An individual, however competent, who must be summoned from some distance, with some delay, is already at a disadvantage in dealing with an emergency. Time spent in transit is time added to development of the emergency and time subtracted from its solution. To put it succinctly, emergencies are often volatile: they are either being dealt with and diminishing, or recognition of their immediacy has been deferred and they are increasing.

Emergency Procedures. Some emergencies, by their nature, cannot be dealt with by one individual, no matter how competent or nearby. Bomb threats and fires, for example, must involve a large percentage of the staff if expeditious evacuation of the building is to be achieved.

An emergency procedures memorandum should detail phone numbers to be called, areas of responsibility, routes of evacuation, and location of emergency equipment. If specific actions are proscribed (for example, during the emergency do *not* turn off lights, do *not* lock doors, do *not* use the elevators, do *not* use the telephones to make personal calls), they should also be included.

What results will, of course, be a rather complex memorandum, since it must deal with different times of day (and different staffing), different kinds of emergencies, and different methods of response. For example, a fire may require the quickest evacuation of the building consistent with safety, while a disturbance outside the building may dictate that the "innocent" be sheltered inside.

The administrator should also submit a memorandum to the fire and police departments (and to the contract security service, if appropriate), giving the names, addresses, and telephone numbers of individuals who should be called in the event of an emergency during hours of closing. For each agency, at least two names should be given.

Other papers which should be immediately available to the staff are accident report forms, insurance forms, and incident report forms.

People Security. It should come as no surprise to the administrator if the staff ranks a well-lighted parking lot higher than an effective collection service, an effective guard above sophisticated locks, a problem-patron procedure above electronic monitoring.

We all want to be secure in our persons, and whatever improves the security of the staff will often enhance the security of the public as well.

Of all the factors against which security methods must be marshaled, the problem patron imparts the greatest perception of insecurity. Clyde W. Grotophorst, in the winter 1979 issue of *Public Library Quarterly,* discusses at length the problem patron and possible responses.[1]

Problem patrons come in all shapes and sizes: from persons who use abusive language to those who abuse drugs, from odoriferous derelicts to unruly teenage gangs, from peepers to psychopaths. Responses and controls are equally varied: from stronger locks to brighter lights, from electronic alarms to uniformed guards.

Guards. To guard or not to guard is not necessarily the question. The giants of the library world may already have their companies or corps of

---

1. Clyde W. Grotophorst, "The Problem Patron: Toward a Comprehensive Response," *Public Library Quarterly* 1:345 (Winter 1979).

guards. The smallest among us may have concluded, long since, that a guard can be employed only at the sacrifice of the essential character of their institution. When the choice comes down to books *or* guard, only one conclusion can be drawn. For all the rest, however, the best advice is: Those that can guard, should.

Some, nevertheless, question the need for a guard. "We are all adults. We deal with the public—some of them demanding or otherwise unpleasant—every day. Why do we need a guard?" The reasons for having a guard are numerous.

1. A uniformed guard—and he or she should be uniformed—provides a visible locus of authority.
2. Staff members need not stop to think to whom an emergency should be referred. The guard was hired for that purpose.
3. The guard will always have, foremost in mind, the rules and regulations of the library and his or her posted orders. Other staff members may have committed procedures for circulation, cataloging, or reference work to memory, but not have ready recall of emergency procedures.
4. The authority of a guard to act in emergencies is strengthened by repeated exercise of that authority. This kind of authority cannot be achieved by a corps of other staff members, acting over an extended time in diverse situations.

However, a guard should not be hired until his or her orders have been developed. The orders should include:

1. All rules, regulations, or guidelines that have been developed for the library.
2. Duty hours, extending perhaps to fifteen minutes past closing, so that the guard may see employees to their cars.
3. Routine. For example, how often a roving guard should visit all parts of the library. When, where, and the duration of breaks and lunch hour.
4. The physical boundaries of the guarded site. For example, is a parking lot included in the guard's regular tour?
5. Phone numbers and individuals to call in the event of an emergency. (In addition, the guard should be provided with a weekly duty roster, listing staff members in charge.)
6. Uniform. For example, are cap and tie mandatory? Are weapons forbidden?
7. Special instructions. For example, the guard should vary his or her tours, so that anyone who might be tempted to vandalize will be unable to predict that, for a certain period of time, the guard will *not* appear.

Three types of guard may be considered: a police officer, an in-house guard, and contract guard services.

Assignment of a police officer as a library guard is becoming less and less common as budgetary problems mount. Moreover, the desirability of exercising that option (where it exists) is open to question for several reasons:

1. It is unlikely that a city's best officer will be assigned to a post that many police captains will regard as a low-crime site.
2. The officer, trained to respond to frequent emergencies, may find the routines dull and the assignment boring, with negative results on effectiveness.
3. The officer—particularly if he or she is subject to emergency calls elsewhere—may be unwilling (or unable) to disarm a dangerous person (especially if library policies call for an unarmed guard).
4. Finally, the officer will tend to act in keeping with his or her police-academy training, thereby eliminating methods of response the administrator might have selected.

Moreover, if an administrator hires an off-duty police officer as a guard, two other factors may come into play. Hours worked beyond the normal schedule usually see a diminishing effectiveness; and the hourly rate of an off-duty police officer will often be approximately twice the rate of a contract-service guard.

The in-house guard is a solution more suited to corporations, colleges and universities, and the largest public libraries than to small and medium-size libraries. Only large entities can have security forces sufficiently large to provide backup for illnesses, vacations, personal emergencies, and twelve-hour (or more) schedules.

A rule of thumb is that to ensure 24-hour coverage for a single guard post, a staff of 4.5 guards is needed. For a six-day, 68-hour library operation, the number drops to about 3. To the salaries of guards the administrator must add (in some cases) fringe benefits, which can increase costs by 25 to 30 percent.

A responsible contract guard service, on the other hand, can be expected to provide backup to cover the full operating schedule of the library, regardless of illnesses, vacations, and personal emergencies; and fringe benefits are absorbed by the company. However, the administrator who decides to hire a contract guard service should keep several points in mind:

1. He or she must be prepared to deal with the four most common problems of contract guard service: inadequate training, poor supervision, low morale, and high turnover. (With diligence, these problems are manageable.)

2. The administrator must bear in mind that he or she is *hiring,* and must insist upon the right to interview and select. (Few library contracts are sufficiently large to influence the agency to assign its best guards automatically.)

3. The administrator must never overvalue the longevity or reputation of the guard service. Neither trait can compensate for an inadequate guard in an emergency.

4. The administrator should seek a guard service contract that specifies the respective liabilities of library and guard service if someone is injured by the action (or failure to act) of the guard. This will not protect the library from being sued, but it can determine who will pay the cost of judgments.

5. The administrator should be aware that, except in special cases (for example, if a guard has the rank of peace officer or is otherwise deputized), a private guard has no more formal authority than an average citizen. The guard's authority devolves from the library's right to protect persons and property. Licensing by the state (where that occurs) is in most instances merely part of the regulatory process and does not grant a guard the powers of a police officer.

6. An administrator should never ask a guard to perform nonguard duties or tasks other than those he or she was hired to perform. Such actions demean the guard or the associated duties, and may influence the regular staff to consider the guard somehow inferior, with unhappy results all around. (It is remarkable, however, how rapidly attitudes change after a guard performs well in a situation that was regarded as threatening by other staff members.)

Manual Alarm Systems. People protection does not—indeed, cannot—always come in human form. Few libraries, save those which combine great wealth with very few service points, are able to provide guards for each of their agencies. For all the rest, the concealed, manual, silent alarm fills a very real need.

By electrical impulse, the silent alarm connects a library employee who may be under duress with the police, a security service, or the answering service of a security service. The manual, silent alarm is often only one component of a more comprehensive system which includes electronic intrusion-detection devices (of which, more later).

The isolation felt in a thinly staffed branch library as a dark winter evening wears on must be experienced to be fully comprehended. Even though the physical isolation persists, reduction of the psychological isolation should receive high administrative priority. The installation of manual, silent alarms is relatively inexpensive, and well worth the cost in terms of staff tranquility.

When installing such a system, the administrator should insist upon the squeeze-type triggering mechanism. It eliminates the possibility that materials pushed onto a shelf, or pulled from it, will accidentally activate the alarm. Nothing upsets police officers more than to be called from official business to answer an alarm that has been accidentally set off. And more than loss of library-employee credibility is involved, since the officer may be cruising busy streets or responding to a real emergency.

Concurrent with installation of a silent alarm system, the administrator should issue guidelines for its use. For example, since its activation will result in police officers' responding,

1. Who should be notified if it is activated: office, switchboard, guard?
2. Should a follow-up call be made to the police as soon as possible?
3. What information should be provided to the police when they arrive—number and description of persons against whom the complaint is lodged, direction of flight, all information and names of witnesses, etc.?
4. Should conditions under which the alarm is to be used be specified —for example, a hold-up, violence or serious threat of violence against persons or property, etc.?

In the last analysis, the security of the people in a library depends upon a staff that is alert and willing to accept responsibility. Nevertheless, addition of a guard and a silent alarm—should the library's budget permit— is recommended. By their effective backup of the staff, they enhance its willingness to be alert and responsible. They will lessen any tendency the staff may have to "look the other way."

Confidentiality of Library Records. Another, more subtle kind of "people security" grows from the library's responsibility to its registered borrowers. The records a library must keep in order to maintain collection security may prompt a person to inquire into what others are reading, and such questions are *prima facie* evidence that the interrogator is up to no good. Any such inquiry must be resisted; and it may be blocked or delayed by administrative memoranda. However, the security of borrowers will be enhanced if the board of trustees adopts an antidisclosure policy statement such as the following:

> It is the policy of the _____ Public Library that circulation records and other records identifying the names of library users are confidential in nature, that the Librarian and all library employees are to maintain the confidentiality of such records and that such records shall not be made available to any person or to any agency of state, federal or local government except pursuant to such process, order or subpoena as may be authorized under the authority of and pursuant to federal, state and local law relating to civil, criminal or administrative discovery pro-

cedures or legislative investigatory power. The Librarian is directed to resist complying with any such process, order or subpoena until such time as a proper showing of good cause has been made in a court of competent jurisdiction. Upon receipt of such a process, order or subpoena the Librarian shall consult with the President, or, in the absence of the President, with another officer of the Library, and shall then determine whether or not consultation with legal counsel is appropriate to determine if such process, order or subpoena is in proper form and if there is a showing of good cause for its issuance. If process, order or subpoena is not in proper form or if good cause has not been shown, they will insist that such defects be cured.[2]

In this way, or by similar means, the most precious security of all—that of intellectual freedom—is strengthened.

Disarming the Armed Staff. One final observation relative to people security: the administrator may have taken every justifiable step to enhance personal security, only to find that his or her staff has gone on ahead—several leagues ahead! Twenty-first-century products are now available, straight out of the James Bond catalog! Individuals can easily procure devices that will stun or incapacitate real or imagined assailants with powerful electric shocks, immensely bright light, or sprays of ortho-chlorobenzalmalononitrile.

To what purpose will an administrator have insisted upon an unarmed guard if members of his or her staff have armed themselves with such exotic weapons, and are ready to use them? It is imperative that the administrator make clear to the staff that weapons of any kind are not to be used while they are on duty. (Portable noise alarms and whistles are not weapons, of course, and are not affected by such a proscription.)

Collection Security

A collection cannot be considered secure unless the status of each item in it can be quickly and accurately reported. Viewed in that light, collection security resolves into degrees of insecurity. Nevertheless, no other area of security has received more attention over the past decade. Developments have been fast and investments high. Developments have been so fast that it is possible to lose sight of the fact that the most important factors determining the security of the collection are the procedures the library has established to govern its use.

2. Hartford Public Library, Board of Directors, *Minutes,* May 21, 1981.

Collection security begins with the procedures for cataloging and circulation, which should tell:

1. If the item is in the library, where can it be found?
2. If it is out of the library, where is it, for what purpose, and when will it be returned?
3. If it is on loan, who has it, at what address, and for what period?
4. If it is on loan and overdue, what steps have been taken to recover it?
5. If it is missing, what steps have been taken to replace it, or to withdraw it from the collection?

Circulation procedures differ so much from library to library (and even within a library system) that extended discussion of them would not be profitable.

Electronic detection systems are the currently popular solution to collection insecurity, and numerous articles report loss reduction by that means of 80 percent or more. However, not everyone is convinced. To put it another way, not everyone is convinced that those who invest in electronic systems have done everything they could or should have done before the installer comes.

Richard W. Boss (in an article in the March 15, 1980, issue of *Library Journal*) discusses the weaknesses of electronic detection systems, and at greater length security problems of structural or procedural nature.[3] (Boss would undoubtedly be the first to admit that not all of the problems are susceptible to administrative remedy.) The burden of the Boss article is (1) know that you have a problem (establish your loss ratio by inventory or sampling) and (2) take the last electronic step only after you have taken the first, nonelectronic steps.

If your library does not have ease of access, your loan period is short and renewals are limited or nonexistent, and many categories of open-shelf books are noncirculating, *you have a problem.*

If your circulation staff does not follow proper procedures, there is no systematic renewal of library cards, and exit control points are staffed by individuals who lack interest and interpersonal skills, *you have a problem.*

If your keys have been widely distributed and much of your inventory has been lost, your property is not marked, your photocopy machines are too few, too expensive, and too often out of order, *you have a problem.*

Even with an electronic detection system, Boss seems to say, you would have a problem. Correct these failings, and then you will deserve, and be able to make the best use of, the electronic solution.

3. Richard W. Boss, "The Library Security Myth," *Library Journal* 105:683 (15 March 1980).

Nevertheless, electronic detection systems are hard to resist. On the one hand, "everyone is doing it." On the other hand, it is a project for which it is easy to write grant applications.

The administrator who is considering such a system will first want to discover if his or her worst suspicions, relative to unauthorized removal of library materials, are fact or fancy. Alice Harrison Bahr, in her *Book Theft and Library Security Systems, 1978–79,* offers a good summary (pages 7 to 28) of methods by which the administrator can make that determination.[4] She discusses book census, inventory, and sampling. Unless the period between initial consideration of the system and decision to purchase is long, the sampling method will probably be preferred and will serve perfectly well.

When sampling is over and the selection process begins, the administrator will want to keep two things in mind. First, to be sure that the electronic detection system under consideration is compatible with any existing (or planned) automated circulation system. For example, the detection system may work well, but nonetheless cause problems when data are entered in the circulation system. Second, to determine whether the bypass or full-circulating system best fits the library's operations layout.

In the bypass mode, materials that are being charged out must be passed around the control gate; in the full-circulating mode, detector strips are deactivated, and the books can then be carried through the control gate. Materials that have not been handled in one of these two ways will cause an alarm to sound (usually) and the control gate to lock. (Note: in the full-circulating mode, new employees have been known to deactivate—and thus erase—cassette tapes.)

Bahr, in the book mentioned above, provides good descriptions of the seven most common electronic detection systems (pages 33 to 76). Nevertheless, an administrator who is seriously considering such a system will want on-site demonstrations by a number of vendors.

Two additional points: negotiations are appropriate, for prices are not cast in concrete; and the ongoing cost of detection strips can mount over a period of time, even if the difference is no more than one cent per strip.

The three basic types of detection systems are magnetic, electromagnetic, and radio frequency. The first of these is more susceptible to false alarms, and the third more suited to bypass than to full-circulating operations.

All three types work; but all three can be fooled. Their great advantage

4. Alice Harrison Bahr, *Book Theft and Library Security Systems, 1978–79* (White Plains, N.Y.: Knowledge Industry Publications, 1978).

is that they remove the personal element from control-gate confrontations. It is the machine—not a staff member—that says, "Excuse me, wait a minute. Do you have something there that you forgot to charge out?"

Rare or Unique Materials. For rare materials, ordinary procedures and high-tech detection systems will not suffice. Timothy Walch, in an article in the March 1977 issue of *College and Research Libraries,* calls attention to the rules established for users of the North Carolina Division of Archives and History.[5] Few libraries would care to adopt the entire procedure; however, it is a good example of the extremes to which an administrator may be pushed in the desire to protect rare and valuable materials. A typical user of the NCDAH goes through the following steps:

1. He or she goes to a security officer in the lobby and presents identification. If the identification is satisfactory, the officer prepares a photo-identification card for the user.
2. Still outside the reference room, the user goes to the coat racks and lockers and leaves any briefcases, attaché cases, overcoats, notebooks, envelopes, etc.—anything in which materials might be concealed.
3. The user then gains admission to the reference room by means of the photo-identification card.
4. After call slips for the material the user wishes to see are prepared, the slips and identification card are turned in to the reference desk.
5. The user is limited to one box of material and is allowed to have only one folder open at a time.
6. Manuscripts or volumes are placed flat on the desk, not tilted on the edge.
7. When the material is returned to the reference desk, the user's identification card is returned.
8. After getting his or her possessions from coat rack or locker, the user returns to the security officer and again shows his or her identification card, before departing.

Walch goes on to suggest indelible stamping of valuable materials; consent-to-search forms, to be signed by users of the collection; inventory of valuable items at least every three years; keeping good records of photocopies and call slips in order to prove ownership; and the bonding of employees in sensitive positions. Even so, he adds, "vigilant reference room surveillance is the nucleus of an effective security program."

Procedures for Apprehending Thieves. Suppose that, as a result of

5. Timothy Walch, "The Improvement of Library Security," *College & Research Libraries* 38:100 (March 1977).

vigilant surveillance or through the good workings of library procedures and/or the electronic detection system, something (it need not be rare and valuable) is perceived to be in the process of unauthorized removal. What is to be done?

It is not enough to know that in most states the destruction or mutilation of library materials, or keeping them past the loan period, is considered a misdemeanor. Nor is it enough to know that if you are in the Commonwealth of Virginia, the mere act of concealing library property on library premises is considered proof that larceny is intended.

There is no substitute for knowing the laws of your state. Is the theft of library materials a misdemeanor? Is it sometimes a felony? Do the shoplifting statutes apply? Can you detain a person for a reasonable period of time? Must you file charges if you do? Must the suspect leave the premises before he or she can be apprehended? Are there circumstances under which a search of the suspect can be made?

Again, there is no substitute for knowing the laws of your state. Even where shoplifting statutes apply, they differ widely from state to state. The security of the library and the employee is at stake, since, unless an infraction is correctly and lawfully handled, a suit for unlawful search, invasion of privacy, or false arrest may ensue.

Once the administrator has determined the application and extent of local and state laws, as they apply to unauthorized removal of library material, it is his or her responsibility to condense and codify them into a form usable by the staff. (Without doubt, their legal language will need explanation and clarification.) Beyond the technical letter of the law, however, the rule of reason must prevail. All criminal acts are not equal before the law, and few of the crimes that occur in libraries will justify use of force by the staff.

Imagine, for example, a staff member tackling on the stairs a patron suspected of stealing a magazine! Such precipitous action could result in a greater "penalty," paid by the patron—as a result of staff action—than any that may be assigned in a court of law. The library, be assured, *will* be held responsible. (Bintliff's and Coco's article in this volume describes those problems in greater detail.)

Alex Ladenson provides a valuable overview of the subject in the March 1977 issue of *College and Research Libraries*.[6] On pages 116–17, Ladenson offers "A Model Law Relating to Library Theft." A good presentation of guidelines for the apprehension and prosecution of shoplifters is offered by Daniel J. Benny in the August 1981 *Security Man-*

6. Alex Ladenson, "Library Security and the Law," *College & Research Libraries* 38:109 (March 1977).

agement.[7] The bookman's point of view regarding rare-book and manuscript theft is well presented by John H. Jenkins in the February 15 1982 *A B Bookman's Weekly.*[8] The rather limited role of the FBI is described by William J. Riley in the March 1977 *College and Research Libraries.*[9]

Building Security

If the administrator talks to the staff, he or she will learn much about the weak points of building security. Nevertheless, a professional survey is recommended. Police and fire departments are often quite willing to offer advice. An insurance company's survey of situations that might cause injury and lead to liability claims is helpful in certain areas, and a fuller survey could be sought from them. An outside consultant, for a fee that perhaps will not exceed $1,500 for a building, will present a full program of building security. Finally, the advice of vendors on building security is very informative and helpful—as long as the administrator is able to assess what advice is based on the requirements of the situation and what is based on marketing.

None of the above—staff, police, fire, insurance appraiser, outside consultant, vendors—absolves the administrator from the obligation of conducting his or her survey of building security. The administrator should look at the building as if he or she were a burglar, about to break in. Seen from that point of view, the library becomes less the impregnable civic fortress and more the vulnerable civic asset, with numerous points of entry. Walls, roofs, and even floors have been breached as if they were doors, windows, skylights, hatches. People must come and go, light must enter the building, and utilities must be provided access.

Whatever is done in the name of building security will not be enough to stop a determined burglar. Nor should the administrator attempt such a feat. His or her task is to select security devices that will complicate, delay, discourage. In any case, the burglar who, so to speak, would use up part of his luck breaking into the average library cannot be considered professional. The library has more to fear from the casual—even whimsical—entry of opportunity by neighborhood misfits. And these are the very ones who are most apt to be discouraged if entry has been com-

7. Daniel J. Benny, "Risky Business," *Security Management* 25/8:46 (Aug. 1981).

8. John H. Jenkins, "Rare Book and Manuscript Thefts," *A B Bookman's Weekly* 69:1224 (15 Feb. 1982).

9. William J. Riley, "Library Security and the Federal Bureau of Investigation," *College & Research Libraries* 38:104 (March 1977).

plicated, the time needed to effect entry lengthened, the chance of detection increased.

The administrator who is still at the planning stage for a new building is fortunate indeed. He or she can incorporate an integrated security system at a cost which probably will not exceed 1 percent of total cost. In that situation, the administrator will want to install and activate the security system at the earliest practicable moment. A building is never more vulnerable, or more attractive to criminals, than when it is nearing completion.

Doors. When thinking of security, one naturally thinks first of locking doors. The characteristics of a well-locked door are known to any competent carpenter or locksmith. The administrator will be advised by them to look for strong, close-fitting, reinforced door jambs (preferably one-piece structural steel); locking bolts, not less than 1 inch in length; hardened metal plates, fastened from the inside and covering the lock area, and/or a slip ring to protect the exterior cylinder; three hinges per door, with concealed hinge screws 2 or 3 inches long and with hinge pins on the inside of the door, where possible (or secured by pins or flanges where not); solid metal doors in insecure areas and solid wood doors, 1¾ inches thick, in other areas; and in some areas manually or key-operated bolts into the upper door jamb and floor. Experts can add many other ideas.

In considering these and other characteristics, the administrator will want to evaluate each in the light of the most common methods of assaulting doors: kicking out hollow-panel doors, prying the door away from the jamb, cutting through the bolt, pulling out the cylinder, drilling through the lock, and knocking off the handle.

The lock should be chosen for more than esthetic reasons. A good-quality, pin-tumbler, cylinder lock will provide good-quality security. Lever locks and disc (wafer) cylinder locks are more suited to desks, files, cabinets, and lockers. Keyless locks—cipher, electronic, card—seem to have limited application in library operations.

Some exterior doors may not be locked at all—from the inside. Laws may require that "panic bars" be installed to permit exiting in an emergency. If such a door is in an area remote from regular surveillance, one solution is to fit it with an alarm which will automatically sound if the door is opened. (Of course, the alarm can be deactivated by a key.) Even though the door so equipped may be too far from service areas to allow the staff to apprehend the individual who is leaving, the alarm serves as a real deterrent. The individual who opens the door is exiting into an unknown (perhaps the police or others in authority are just outside the door?) with a noisy alarm sounding overhead.

Once the good, solid door has been secured by the good, quality lock, protection would seem assured, unless control of the keys has been lost! Is the key inventory up to date? Do only those who *must* have the keys have them? Have the locks been rekeyed since the previous cleaning crew was replaced? The hardware may be great but the security miserable, simply because control of the keys has been lost.

Windows. Unless it is as high as an elephant's eye (i.e., at least 18 feet from the ground), a window must be considered a hazard. In older buildings, a high percentage of windows open for ventilation, and few lock with keys. If light and not ventilation is needed, "glass brick" is a secure alternative. Chain-operated jalousie windows are relatively secure.

In some areas, the administrator will want to substitute other products for "plate glass" (which may be reinforced by lamination) or replace it with a plastic product. Plastic is often three times as expensive as glass and half again as expensive as laminated glass; however, it is, as advertised, many, many more times resistant to impact. Unfortunately, it is relatively soft, so that graffiti can be cut into it and open flame can disfigure it. In addition (the reverse of its chief advantage), it is *so* impact resistant that the individual who persists in forcing such a window will often destroy the window frame in the process.

At ground level or below, one should consider covering the windows with grating—even welding it in place over exterior windows. For maximum security of grating or fencing, the administrator may wish to consider the more expensive expanded metal. (Information may be obtained from the Expanded Metal Manufacturers' Association, Suite 2026, 221 N. LaSalle Street, Chicago, Ill. 60601.)

Fire Detection and Suppression Equipment. When contemplating fire hazards, what the administrator will choose to do—indeed, *can* do—depends primarily on local and state codes. Some codes, for example, may require—at least in new buildings—a comprehensive sprinkler system. Fortunately, the new sprinkler systems are not the uncertain menace their predecessors sometimes were, where minor fires resulted in major damage when sprinklers were activated over a large area. Today, sprinkler systems "water down" only the area of the fire.

Since local and state codes will govern, what follows are only suggestions about how devices might be applied.

1. Sprinkler systems—in areas where combustibles are concentrated: print shop, cleaning supplies, loose paper products

2. Rate-of-rise heat detectors—in staff room, where cooking may be done, and in restrooms where smokers may gather

3. Smoke detectors—in duct work, to shut down duct fans or air conditioner and thus prevent circulation of smoke throughout the building

4. Ionization detectors—throughout the building. Their sensitivity permits them to detect particles of combustion *before* smoke or open flame can be seen. (Any building-wide system, ionization or other, can be connected to a display board which will indicate the section of the building in which a sensor has been activated. This is a great help when the public is running out of the building and firemen are running in!)

5. Halon fire-suppression system—Halon is a liquid that, under pressure, forms a gas that can quickly extinguish a fire without damage to life or property. Applications: protection of rare and valuable materials and an automatic data-processing center.

6. Portable fire extinguishers—distributed (preferably) no more than 50 feet from any location in the building. The universal ABC type is usually to be preferred (though more expensive) to the types (A, B, and C) intended for more specialized use. For example, a type A extinguisher (using soda and acid to develop the pressure to drive water from the tank) could actually spread, and thus worsen, an oil fire, and if used on an electrical fire could result in a nasty shock for the firefighter. In any case, the administrator must emphasize to the staff that extinguishers are to be used only *after* the fire department has been called.

Whatever program is adopted must be related to the anticipated response time of the fire department. For example, ionization detectors, whose chief virtue is that they provide the earliest information that a fire is about to erupt, may not be sufficient if the response time of the fire department is long. A supplementary fire-suppression system may then be needed.

Data-Processing Center Security. The security of the automatic data-processing center may be enhanced with a Halon fire-suppression system, but it begins in a clean environment, controlled as to temperature and humidity. Within that environment, the security of the center depends on the procedures the library has established to prevent unauthorized manipulation, modification, destruction, or disclosure of data.

These security steps are suggested in *Industrial Security Manual for Safeguarding Classified Information* of the Department of Defense (July 1981):

1. Limitation of access and visitor control.

2. Protection for both hardware and software when not in use.

3. Storage and protection for data base input materials and output products.

4. Establishment of start-up, shut-down, and re-start procedures.

5. Code-identified access to the data base, and only to that part of the data base to which the individual is entitled.

6. Establishment of conditions under which the data base may be augmented or modified.

7. Enforcement of procedures for those who test and maintain—not just those who use—the system.[10]

Intrusion-Detection Devices. Three types of detection devices will *not* be considered here. The first of these is the bell-ringer alarm, which can be described as more of a neighborhood nuisance than a device that will incite to useful, timely action. Second are the photoelectric devices, which are seldom considered today for sensitive areas; however, they continue to serve well as patron counters (but so do gates and pressure mats) and as decoys for the actual, concealed detectors. The third is closed-circuit TV. It is sometimes the best answer, but almost always the most expensive answer. In any case, as it might be applied in a library situation, CCTV functions more as a method of extending normal surveillance than as a burglar alarm.

Other detection devices may be classified as providing either area or perimeter protection. For many decades we have all been familiar with one form of perimeter protection: foil strips around every door, every window, every skylight and hatchway. (With this type of protection, no point of entry is unprotected.) Break the foil and you have broken the circuit, and the next sound you will hear is the approaching police siren. Few library administrators are in a position to consider perimeter protection, because it is expensive to install and expensive to maintain. Neither the electronic nor the open or closed electrical circuit installations can be provided at a cost compatible with the budgets of nonprofit institutions. (Fences, as fixed perimeter protection, are of course another matter.)

Turning to area-protection devices, the administrator will consider two basic types: those that generate energy, then detect reflections of it (e.g., microwave and ultrasonic), and those that "passively" detect changes in background levels of energy, for example, audio (sonic) and thermal (passive infrared, or **PIR**).

Whatever may be claimed by the manufacturers or sales representatives, most of these systems have an effective scanning area of 500 to 1,500 square feet. (One exception is the audio detection system, which may record a sonic boom created several thousand feet above the sensor!)

In any case, the administrator will select protective devices for only a part—perhaps only a very small part—of the building, concentrating on valuable equipment, rare books, automatic data-processing center, etc.

10. U.S. Dept. of Defense, *Industrial Security Manual for Safeguarding Classified Information* (Washington, D.C.: Government Printing Office, 1981). (DoD 5220.22-M).

The manual, silent alarm (mentioned under "People Security") can be integrated with most of these systems. With intrusion-detection alarms, even more than with the manual, silent alarm, the purpose is to reach someone (security company, police) *outside* the building. The manual, silent alarm is activated when the employee perceives that he or she is unable to cope with an explosive situation. Perhaps they *might* have coped, given time. However, when a burglar alarm is activated, the staff is gone and the building is empty and vulnerable.

All of these systems work. Police departments would say that they work *too* well, since 90 percent of their burglar-alarm calls prove to be false alarms. One recent survey (conducted for the National Institute of Justice by Hallcrest Systems, Inc., in 1981) revealed that 57 percent of the law enforcement officers surveyed favored transfer of burglar-alarm response to private security. (Who can blame them?)

The installer will protect the administrator from making obvious mistakes. For example, the passive infrared detector is known to be immune to most causes of false alarms, but it should not be aimed at an object (say a heating register) that might show a sudden change of temperature. The mistakes that cause problems are human mistakes. Did the cleaning crew forget to turn off the system before starting work? Or forget to turn the system back on before leaving? Did someone leave a window open, and is the blowing blind now registering as a burglar?

The biggest mistake of all, however, is to take the system for granted. Weekly checking of the system, at all locations, is a must.

The only practical solution for the administrator is to adopt *one* burglar alarm system for the entire library. In that way, one vendor will be responsible and one method of operation in effect. (The cost of the system should also be lower than if it were divided among two or more vendors.) Nevertheless, the administrator should be aware that the degree of security will vary from location to location. One branch library may be in a secure, low-crime neighborhood, another in a high-crime neighborhood. A Small Business Administration survey found that while 21 percent of all small businesses had suffered at least one property insurance problem during the previous year, 43 percent of retail stores in ghettos had.[11]

One should note that the presentation on protection devices in the March 1977 *Library Technology Reports* is still germane and valuable.[12]

Interior Layout. Building security does not stop with methods (locks, window screens, burglar alarms) that deny or complicate unauthorized

11. U.S. Small Business Administration, *Crime against Small Business* (Washington, D.C.: Government Printing Office, 1969).

12. *Library Technology Reports* (March 1977).

entrance. The interior layout of a building can either encourage or discourage crime. For example, high fixtures and dim lighting encourage crime. If service desks are placed for optimum supervision, they discourage crime. Book stacks so high that they obstruct the view encourage crime.

Operating Procedures. As building security improves, emphasis will shift to operating procedures. For example, the better the locks, window screens, lights, and burglar alarms, the more necessary the observance of proper entrance, exit, and lock-up procedures. And if service is offered and given quickly, theft is less apt to occur. Moreover, in greeting the borrower, the employee pierces the anonymity that is important to anyone with a criminal bent.

An up-to-date inventory of all furniture and equipment is essential. Near or next to the library's inventory number (which should be attached to the item) should appear a full description of the item (enough to identify it), with model and serial numbers. If, for example, a minicomputer is stolen and the police want to enter it in the FBI's National Crime Information Center computer, they will ask for an SN number (manufacturer's serial number) and an OAN number (owner applied—i.e., inventory—number)—in addition to manufacturer, model, color, etc. Except in special circumstances (e.g., lease or short-term ownership), the administrator should consider stenciling or engraving equipment with the library's name, a practice that is known to reduce resale value substantially.

A final note on procedures, as they relate to building security, has to do with the handling of money. No one expects to get rich robbing libraries; nevertheless, if an unusual number of copies is made, an unusual number of lost books are paid for, a scheduled bank deposit is missed, a surprising amount of money can be at risk. Therefore, the administrator should keep cash on hand to the minimum needed to begin the next day's operations. This is accomplished by scheduling frequent bank deposits. Also, at the close of each day, the money should be taken out of copying machines and cash register (and both left open) and deposited in the safe. The safe should be bolted to the counter, and be protected by an area-type burglar alarm during the hours of closing.

Site Security

An administrator should also view the library from afar. From six blocks out, at each principal point of compass, is it clear where the library is, and can one get there from here? In this regard, the new symbol signs of the American Library Association can be helpful, saying: "The library is in this direction" or "the library is in that direction," or "this *is* the library." Granted that this security is somewhat ambiguous; nevertheless, studies have shown that individuals who stride purposefully toward a known destination are less apt to be accosted or mugged. And we want all borrowers to make it all the way to the library!

The administrator's responsibility begins before the patron sets foot on library property. Are the streets around the library properly lighted? Is a stop light (or stop sign) needed? Are the crosswalks clearly marked? Are the curbs cut to accommodate the handicapped and the bicycles of young people? Is the bus stop conveniently near the front door of the library? Are the sidewalks in good repair? Is a fire hydrant nearby—and a fire-alarm box, if the library lacks an internal fire-alarm system? Are signs for a reduced speed zone posted, if necessary? Etc., etc.

All of these things must be accomplished by working with and through others. Nevertheless, it is the library administrator's job to initiate action. In the words of a philosopher, "If not him or her, then whom?"

Lighting. Good lighting of the exterior of the building is of primary importance—not for crime detection but for crime prevention. Evenness of light, with no bright spots or dark shadows, is most desirable. Its purpose is to reveal the criminal, and illegal acts, without spotlighting potential victims. To achieve this, it is well to consider the type and level of ambient lighting. For example, if the nearby street has high-pressure sodium lighting and the library has mercury vapor lighting, the shadows cast next to the building may seem all the darker.

The library parking lot (if any) should be lighted as brightly as the building.

A "side benefit" of good lighting is that guards (if any) may patrol more frequently and more thoroughly.

Other desirables of site security are a building that

1. Stands alone (an intruder cannot gain access from an adjacent building).
2. Is light in color (so that the outline of an intruder can be clearly seen).
3. Is situated on relatively low, light-colored ground.
4. Has no adjacent telephone pole nor any large tree closer than 40 feet.
5. Has no ground cover or shrubbery taller than 2 feet.
6. Has no blind alleys (where a person could be trapped or a burglar work undisturbed).
7. Has exterior fire escapes that provide for quick exit but difficult entry.

Miscellaneous

School, academic, and special libraries differ from public libraries in many particulars. They differ as to *buildings*. In virtually every case, school and special libraries are within the building or *are* a building of the parent institution. Academic libraries are apt to be separate buildings, within an institutional complex. In every case, security measures will either be identical with or extensions of overall institutional security.

They differ as to *collections*. School and academic collections must respond to curricula imperatives. Some may have developed very fine general collections, but always in addition to—rather than at the expense of—the needs of the curriculum. Special library collections must be pertinent to the corporate needs which justify their existence. Those needs may even dictate the form the collection takes. In turn, the form may require special security requirements. For example, the special librarian whose collection emphasizes software or terminals for access to remote data banks will have a different perception of security needs than the librarian whose collection is largely books and periodicals.

They differ as to *clientele*. School, academic, and special libraries, acting as "sole vendor" or "vendor of choice" to their clientele, have a degree of control that is lacking in public libraries. A public librarian's threat to withdraw borrowing privileges lacks the convincing ring of "Do you want to graduate?" or "Do you want to keep your job?" Granted, this is a rather nebulous form of security; nevertheless, the relationship is exploitable (up to a point).

Of course, special controls imply special responsibilities. The school librarian cannot be unaware of his or her institution's responsibility to act *in loco parentis* as regards school library clientele. At the college and university level, the responsibility may be lessened in general but heightened in particular, for example, in on-campus dormitories and 24-hour libraries.

Vandalism, with certain spectacular exceptions, seems to be more a problem for school libraries (and schools) than for other types of libraries. The student whose work or personal qualities have been judged subpar by a school is more apt to "strike back" than the student who faces a public library's overdue fine.

Where vandalism is not an attempt to destroy the institution or part of it, it frequently appears as graffiti. One may suggest that where graffiti appears, security has already been breached. An unpleasant axiom of graffiti is "the more we have, the more we get."

Fortunately, graffiti is no longer the unsolvable (indissoluble) problem it once was. Improved methylene chloride gels for removal of spray paints and new, impermeable coatings (*not* the old urethane, acrylin, and epoxy barrier coatings) have taken some of the venom out of this anti-social act. However, some inks and nonsolvent paints still resist virtually all attempts at removal (short of sand-blasting away the surface).[13]

Guards in schools, colleges, and universities are in a somewhat different situation than their brethren in public libraries. Like their public library counterparts, they are rarely sworn police officers, with powers of arrest and adjudication. Nevertheless, in dealing every day with the same faculty and students, they are in a position to spot the intruder who is bent on mischief. In colleges and universities, they frequently deal with students who are provided with photo-ID cards.

College and university guards, in particular, should prepare themselves to deal amicably and effectively with their city-police counterparts on town-and-gown problems (e.g., the college student who is passing bad checks in town, the "locals" engaged in theft or trespass on the campus).

Planning for the Handicapped. One security task that is often resented is planning for the handicapped. "Look at all the expense and trouble we have gone to for just a handful of individuals!" The individual who says that is often thinking of a person in a wheelchair, and it is true that he or she may seldom be seen in the library. However, many more than those who are confined to a wheelcair are handicapped, and most of us are handicapped (to a degree) at various times in our lives. When we are, we may benefit from—and bless—a barrier-free library.

Think of heart-attack victims, pregnant women, people carrying unwieldy packages, people with arthritic limbs and knees, young children. For them, security consists largely of a library that has not put difficult obstacles in their way.

Identification. Identification badges, if they are worn, should be worn by *all* the staff, including the administrator. The badges serve both the staff ("I wonder if that stranger in the elevator is a new employee?") and the public ("That woman seems to know what she is doing, but does she work here? Can I ask her to help?"). Nevertheless, there are wide differences of opinion on the desirability of badges, and this must be settled on a library-by-library basis.

As Others See Us

1. From Cameron Gerlach's article in the November 1979 issue of the *Smithsonian:* "Maybe a third of the thefts from libraries are—and always have been—inside jobs, sometimes the work of part-time or tem-

13. "How to Control Graffiti," *American School and University* 54:50 (Nov. 1981).

porary staff, but more often of long-timers, for years disgruntled at being underpaid."[14]

2. From John H. Jenkins' article in the February 15, 1982, issue of *A B Bookman's Weekly*: Library and archival security is "usually lax regarding employees and staff members. They may have elaborate security concerning patrons, but inadequate security for employees—who are the persons placed in greatest temptation."[15]

3. From Ivan Hill's article in the July 1981 issue of *Security Management*: "A large number of us seem content in the belief that as long as we observe reasonable ethical standards, we do not need to feel responsible for the conduct of others. . . . Ethics is the lifeblood of a free society, and it can tolerate only so much adulteration. . . . Without a strong foundation of ethics, laws cannot be effective. So much major crime happens as a result of our condoning and implicitly accepting most minor dishonesty."[16]

Everything that is said above has been developed from a view of security as broad as Webster's: "(1) Freedom from danger, risk, etc.; safety. (2) Feedom from care, apprehension, or doubt; well-founded confidence." In short, the proposed measures are intended to evoke a feeling of well-founded confidence in both the public and the library staff. The final words on the subject, however, are credited by Pamela James (*Security Management,* March 1981) to one Bill Norman: "The first thing to know in preparing to carry out a security survey is that no one has published a survey that will meet the requirements of your facility."[17]

Table of Contents for a Security Procedures Manual

Since security is an ongoing process and problem, the in-house security-procedures manual begins to go out of date the moment it is issued. Any change in personnel, schedule, equipment, or community can effect one or more changes in the manual. Even a perception by the staff

14. Cameron Gerlach, "Your Neighbor in the Library May Be a Thief," *Smithsonian* 10/8:140 (Nov. 1979).

15. See note 8 above.

16. Ivan Hill, "Common Sense and Everyday Ethics," *Security Management* 25/7:123 (July 1981).

17. Pamela James, "Casing the Joint," *Security Management* 25/3:38 (March 1981).

that changes have occurred (for example, in the community) can dictate changes in procedures.

The staff security-procedures manual should contain at least the following information.

1. Telephone Numbers
    a. Of all staff, with "telephone tree" memorandum, for calls concerning emergency closings or delayed openings
    b. Of contact individuals (at least two for each agency) for emergencies which occur when library is closed, for police and guard service
    c. Of numbers which should be called if emergencies occur when library is open
2. List of those authorized to act for the library (listed in priority order and defining circumstances when "duty officer" is authorized to act)
3. Rules and regulations of the library
4. Guard instructions
5. Emergency evacuation procedures (including telephone numbers to call, areas of responsibility, location of emergency equipment, routes of evacuation, etc.)
6. Accident report forms and instructions
7. Incident report forms
8. Bomb-threat-caller-characteristics form
9. Civil defense instructions (if appropriate)
10. List of approved vendors (e.g., if window is broken or heating unit malfunctions when administration is not available)
11. Administrative guidelines, as appropriate (e.g., handling of problem patrons)

All of the above items are subject to periodic scheduled review—some at least annually (e.g., 3); some quarterly (e.g., 2); others as needed (e.g., 1). However, in addition, certain security equipment or procedures should be scheduled in the administrative office's pending file or be subject to automatic review:

1. Electronic detection system, circulation desk (checked at least daily)
2. Alarm system, both manual and automatic sensor system (checked weekly)
3. Emergency lights (checked at least bimonthly)
4. Battery-operated door alarms (checked at least bimonthly)
5. Staff security (e.g., problem patrons) meeting (scheduled at least semiannually)

6. Fire extinguishers (checked at least annually)
7. Fire sensors (entire system checked at least biennially)

The foregoing lists are not intended to be comprehensive. They simply indicate the kinds of things a security-minded administrator will attempt to monitor.

JANELLE A.
PARIS

INTERNAL AND EXTERNAL RESPONSIBILITIES AND PRACTICES FOR LIBRARY SECURITY

Few, if any, libraries today are exempt from theft, collection mutilation, arson, graffiti epidemics, vandalism, and other people-provoked abuses. They are also subject to less frequent, but often more devastating, natural disasters: floods, storms, and fires. All of these threats, both human and natural, pose a perilous menace to library personnel and patrons alike. They severely compound the library administrator's responsibilities.

It is the purpose of this article to examine examples of security protection practiced by school, university, and public libraries to stay the tide of these hazards and, specifically, to compare "inside" measures of protection versus "outside" ones.

Inside protection is defined, in this paper, as in-house security services and precautions supplied by members of the library staff, volunteers whom they recruit, or individuals on the library payroll. *Outside protection* refers to surveillance and security provided by police persons (municipal and campus), as well as by companies and agencies that are independent from the library and are contracted for their services.

School Libraries

School libraries, characteristically, are much smaller than academic and public libraries. Furthermore, they usually serve a limited group of patrons. However, size does not ensure safety. School libraries are not immune from problems of security. In fact, they are particularly vulnerable to theft, resource mutilation, nonreturn of materials, prankish mischief, graffiti, disfigurement of property, arson, and vandalism.

In the past few decades, as school libraries have evolved into media centers, their resources have become more expansive, expensive, and sophisticated. The addition of nonbook media, audiovisual equipment, electric typewriters and word processors, media production laboratories, video and television studios, microcomputers, and dial-access informational retrieval systems has tremendously increased the capital investment value of most school library media centers. They are now more attractive targets for thieves and vandals, and the threat posed by fires and storms is of increasing concern. There is obviously greater need for establishing and/or improving security protection.

Although school libraries face the same stressful security situations as other types of libraries, there are some situations affecting security protection that are unique to the school.

The majority of school libraries are understaffed, and many are one-person operations. It is a physical impossibility for one individual to provide the surveillance needed to prevent theft of materials and equipment, mutilation of resources, ripped-out periodical pages, removal of batteries from cassette players, graffiti inscriptions on furniture and walls, and the selling of drugs in restrooms. If policing becomes the number-one priority, library users are the losers. They are deprived of the help, guidance, and direction of the well-trained school media specialist. Although skillful in meeting information needs of the patrons, most media specialists have little or no background experience in dealing with crime and security problems. It is a catch-22 situation.

Another consideration that affects the security aspects of the school media center is the immaturity of student-library patrons. Although their ages may range from 3 years (early childhood education) to 18 or 19 years, the library users are still preadults and subject to youthful indiscretions. Media specialists' patience and ingenuity are often taxed by prankish mischief. While not particularly destructive or dangerous, the pranks often result in loss of time and effort, and may cost money to rectify. And of course, some pranks can be real security hazards, causing bodily harm or material destruction. Through lack of wisdom and for "the fun of it," students may remove shelf clips, steal library signs, rearrange cards in the catalog, sign other students' names on circulation cards, drop stink bombs in the book return, and stuff paperbacks down the commodes. Many receive their "kicks" from trying to "beat the system." They often brag to their peers when they have taken uncharged resources from the school media center.

Many student media-center users are not voluntary patrons. Some are scheduled for periodic visits on a regular basis; others are scheduled for class-related assignments irregularly. This involuntary status may contribute to some of the nuisance-type pranks. Uninterested students are apt to use their time plotting and planning mischief.

Among each student body there are also brazen thieves and destructive vandals. Persons under the age of 25 accounted for more than 50 percent of arrests in the United States in 1981, according to U.S. Department of Justice statistics.[1] Twenty-one percent of the Crime Index offenses cleared in 1981 involved persons under the age of 18.[2] It comes, then, as no surprise that schools are high-risk institutions.

Schools and libraries are susceptible to criminal attacks by former students, dropouts, and those on temporary suspension. Some of these sprees may be motivated by grudges against the school system. The library and the book are often viewed as symbols of education, making them targets for angry disillusionment. Vandalism can leave in its wake smashed furniture, torn-apart books, spray-painted walls, and demolished equipment. Worse yet, the arsonist's torch can destroy the entire library or school. School-library media centers may inadvertently suffer damage that spills over from neighboring areas. They are often in close proximity to the school's administration offices, which may be the focus of the vandalism or arson.

Architectural design and sheer expanse of floor space increase the difficulty of implementing security measures in many school media centers. Some libraries have many entrances, blind corners, stack areas that do not permit easy supervision. Many lack storage rooms with locks to provide security for expensive equipment. The "blueprint stage" is of course the time to plan for security, for often it is difficult to transform a ready-built media center into a safe, security-controlled center. Open-concept schools and media centers without walls can introduce multiple security problems, particularly collection erosion.

Resources in new formats may share some of the blame for acceleration of thefts in school media centers. Today, in many libraries, there is an increase in the use of paperbacks. These books are easier to conceal than hardback copies, thus easier to steal. To many patrons, they are not "real" books and are considered fair game for pilfering. Cassette tapes are also theft prone. Pocket-sized, they are easy to slip out the media center door.

1. U.S. Department of Justice, Federal Bureau of Investigation, *Uniform Crime Reports for the United States* (Washington, D.C., Government Printing Office, 1982), p. 160.
2. Ibid., p. 151.

Inside Security Protection. School media centers, in comparison with public and academic libraries, are low-budget operations. Rarely are funds available for improving security protection through the addition of either expensive equipment or staff. Most efforts to weld the weak links of security fall upon the limited number of staff members to handle in-house provisions. Some of the steps that are frequently taken by media center personnel to curtail theft, discourage resources mutilation, retrieve long-overdue materials, and provide increased security protection are:

1. Increase accessibility of resources. It is thought that many thefts result from difficulty in initially obtaining desired items; thus stealing is prompted by frustration buildup. Also, it is sometimes noted that libraries with high theft statistics are apt to have the most stringent restrictions. To increase collection accessibility, media center admittance, registration, acquisition, circulation, and usage policies should be analyzed for possible modification, keeping in mind the needs of the users. Some points of accessibility to consider are:

   a. Simple registration procedures for new users
   b. Quick and efficient checkout
   c. Convenient library hours
   d. Adequate loan periods
   e. Few restrictions on number of items checked out
   f. Renewal of all items, except those on reserve
   g. Personal reserve system for titles in circulation
   h. Circulation of curriculum reserves at least overnight
   i. Circulation of some reference and nonbook titles
   j. Long-range classroom loans
   k. Interloan policy for titles not available
   l. Selection policy that reflects users' needs
   m. Collection that strongly supports the curriculum
   n. Flexible and adequate scheduling for individual and class use
   o. Multiple copies of high-demand items
   p. Adequate holdings of both current and back-issue periodicals
   q. Paperback editions in popular subject areas
   r. Microfilm files for some periodical backfiles
   s. No-fine policy for overdues
   t. Inexpensive photocopying services
   u. Typewriters for student use

2. Build rapport with library users and improve public relations. A friendly, relaxed atmosphere in the school media center can create a healthy climate and help rapport between staff and users. Many persons believe that improved public relations is one key to the reduction of se-

curity threats, particularly theft. Cathie Hilterbran, conductor of a study of book losses in Ohio public school media centers in 1979, concluded:

> The most important solution to the problem [book losses] is in public relations. Physical controls are never successful without some inherent regard for public property. Media centers must shift the focus from emphasizing physical restraints to public relations and to changing student attitudes. Making students a part of the system instead of "the other side" will do more toward reducing book loss than any detection system. . . . Public relation efforts are time consuming and the results are often slow and difficult to detect, but in the long run public relations and not physical restraints will cut book losses.[3]

Another survey of book loss in a school setting was made by Marvis Canon at the University School at Indiana State University, also in 1979. An attitudinal questionnaire, given to 217 elementary and junior high school students, was included in the study. Canon summarized her findings with the following statement: "Although security systems may reduce book loss temporarily, they do not cure the underlying causes. The prevention of book loss lies in procedural and attitudinal changes."[4]

The following are points to consider in building a favorable image for the media center and strengthening relations with users:

a. Pleasant, attractive, inviting atmosphere in media center
b. Friendly, courteous service at the circulation desk
c. More floor work, asking frequently if help is needed
d. Nonthreatening attitude toward patrons with overdues
e. Shelf checking before sending overdue notices
f. All library policies in writing
g. Uniform application of policies
h. Suggestion box for student input
i. Use of school-wide photo-identification cards for book circulation
j. Good signs in library
k. Relevant recreation materials
l. "Give-away files" and "cutting shelves" of weeded periodicals and newspapers
m. Creative alternatives to fines
n. Innovative library programming

3. Cathie Hilterbran, "Theft Losses in Ohio School Media Centers," *Ohio Media Spectrum* 33:38 (1981).
4. Marvis Canon, "Book Loss: Theft or Apathy," *Indiana Media Journal* 2:25 (Summer 1980).

3. Experiment with methods to combat nonreturn of media center materials. Another grave concern of school media specialists is the "truancy" of library materials. Nonreturn of resources, checked out in good faith, is theft by deception. A high percentage of nonreturned media each year is not only detrimental to collection development, but the retrieval of long-overdue materials can tax the energy and ingenuity of the media specialist. Many librarians advocate a fine-free policy, declaring that it promotes a more positive service image for the library. Some believe that young users are encouraged to return materials, for the right reasons, with a fine-free system.

A number of media specialists are experimenting with ideas to encourage prompt return of materials. For example, some libraries hold raffle programs periodically. Only students with "clear" library records are eligible to draw for a variety of prizes: paperback books, gift certificates from hamburger stands, etc. Some librarians have declared "amnesty" days or weeks to bring in overdue materials. Singing commercials or "promos" can be used as humorous reminders of overdues. This method utilizes familiar tunes with new words about the return of library items. These can be sung over the intercom for the whole school, or hand-picked students can stroll through the halls singing the lyrics and strumming their guitars. One school broadcasts students singing the songs over the school's closed-circuit television. Film showings, parties, traveling banners, and library slumber parties have been tried by desperate librarians to spotlight home rooms that are free from overdues. Rewards are sometimes offered for any books on a "most wanted" list, with no questions asked. Some schools permit "locker checks," or declare periodic locker clean-up days. Report cards are withheld, in some schools, until overdue records have been cleared.

4. Provide door checks. Many libraries hope to reduce unauthorized removal of library resources by searching students' possessions as they leave the media center. By establishing door checks, Plymouth (Wisconsin) High School's losses were reduced by almost 600 books in one year.[5]

If the library is a one-person operation, it is virtually impossible for the media specialist to assist users adequately and also guard the exit. This method is not only time consuming and a deplorable misuse of professional skill, it undermines rapport with students. It also has a tendency to encourage some users to try to "slip one past old eagle eye." In the interest of preserving time, some school media specialists spot-check at the door on an irregular basis. This random inspection may help

5. "Security Systems in Use: Wisconsin Libraries/Media Centers Show Good Results," *Wisconsin Library Bulletin* 76:134 (May–June 1980).

keep some students honest, but it is demeaning both to the media specialist and the library users.

In larger media centers with additional staff, library aides are frequently assigned to serve as guards or monitors to check students at the door. This use of staff personnel for "watchdog" duties removes the worker from performing other tasks of primary importance and could contribute to less efficient service in other areas. Adult volunteers from the community (parents, grandparents, retired teachers, etc.) are utilized in some schools to assist with security checks. Volunteer help is often unreliable, irregular, and of short endurance. The turnover rate is usually exceeded only by the number of "no shows."

Many secondary schools have student-assistant programs in their media centers, and one of the jobs that may be assigned to student workers is that of "door check," which is not popular with pupils. They resent being placed in the position of spying on their peers. Antagonism may flare when they attempt to examine fellow students' possessions. It is difficult, too, for some student assistants to resist favoritism toward their friends. Some of the ones they wave through the exit may be carrying stolen items. The student helpers themselves are not beyond suspicion. In some schools that permit locker inspection, large caches of library materials have been uncovered in student assistants' lockers.

Another reason for failure of the student door guard is time. The short interval between classes is probably the peak period for theft. Student assistants are forced to leave their posts at this time to move to their next class, leaving the door unattended until the next student worker arrives.

5. Improve the physical arrangement to facilitate supervision and to eliminate safety hazards. Many in-house precautionary steps can be taken to lessen the various threats to security. Some simple and inexpensive measures to reduce the likelihood of theft, arson, and vandalism, both during and after library hours, are as follows:

a. Restrict entrances and exits to one door.
b. Place the circulation desk close to the exit.
c. Provide convenient materials-return drop.
d. Use fireproof receptacle to receive materials from interior book drop.
e. Close book drops when the library closes. (Acid, beer, ice cream, mud, water, eggs, firecrackers, etc., have all been known to be deposited in book drops.)
f. Arrange stacks to give an unobstructed view of each aisle.
g. Schedule use of conference rooms and meeting rooms, rather than permitting free access.

   h. Engrave all audiovisual hardware (some suggest in two places) with library identification and serial numbers.

   i. Stamp all materials in several conspicious places with ownership mark.

   j. Empty photocopying machines of money at the end of the day and leave them open.

   k. Restrict the number of persons handling petty cash, maintenance of the copy machine, etc.

   l. Bolt typewriters, microcomputers, etc., to desks.

   m. Paint restrooms a dark color to discourage graffiti.

   n. Consider adding convex security mirrors.

   o. Change locks on library doors so media center will be independent of the master-key system.

   p. Consider exchanging locks periodically with another school.

6. Install electronic security system. The use of theft detection systems has been an effective deterrent to larceny in many media centers. However, its cost makes it impractical for many schools, except those with a very high rate of loss and the financial resources to provide for both the initial investment and the continuing maintenance. Only 5 of 167 Ohio schools surveyed in 1979 used automatic detection systems.[6] A survey among selected Texas school media specialists, also in 1979, revealed that none of the 52 respondents had installed electronic security systems.[7] However, many recorded instances attest to lower theft rates through the use of a detection system. Six Canadian libraries (secondary schools and college levels) had 70 to 94 percent reductions in losses after the installation of detection devices.[8] The average decrease in book loss was 80 percent among high school media centers in the Intermountain West that employed such systems.[9] Alice Bahr cites the average range of loss reduction as 70 to 95 percent with the use of security systems.[10]

No electronic system can stop planned, calculated theft. At best, the systems can prevent casual, spur-of-the-minute theft and "accidental theft" by absent-minded patrons. Some librarians claim that although

---

   6. Hilterbran, "Theft Losses," p. 38.

   7. Janelle A. Paris, "School Library Theft," *Library & Archival Security* 3:33 (Spring 1980).

   8. Sharon Mott, "An Edmonton High School Reduces Book Losses," *Canadian Library Journal* 35:45 (Feb. 1978).

   9. DiAnna Davis, *The Economical Feasibility of Installing a Book Detection System at Cottonwood High School,* ERIC Document 144 603 (1977), p. 3.

   10. Alice Harrison Bahr, *Book Theft and Library Security Systems, 1978–79* (White Plains, N.Y.: Knowledge Industry Publications, 1978), p. 5.

the theft rate decreases after installation of electronic detectors, the mutilation rate climbs. Others have difficulty in utilizing the system with nonbook items. False signals are another source of dissatisfaction with electronic security systems. Most school media centers will continue to experiment with a variety of alternative in-house theft-prevention measures.

Outside Security Protection. It is not economically feasible for the majority of school media centers to seek solutions to security problems through the use of hired "outside" security professionals. Contract guard services would be advantageous in large urban media centers; however, the cost is a major obstacle. More often, the media center utilizes the services of a police person who is shared with other areas of the school. The library receives frequent visits from this individual, as it is part of the patrol route. Visits can be timed to coincide with trouble-prone hours, such as lunch periods and just before and after school. The police person is on immediate call, should an incident require his or her attention. When the media center has extended hours (remaining open at night, for example), the need for police protection increases. Parking lot control is also needed. Off-duty police may be hired to cover media center hours and special programs or functions at night.

Schools in Broward County, Florida, have introduced a good plan. Police make random visits to the closed schools during the night. By mutual agreement between the school administrators and the police, a school was used as a temporary headquarters each night. The police personnel needed a place to write their reports, and the library or school office served this purpose. The required patrol reports were prepared there, in lieu of the police returning to their station. This, of course, provided extensive security for the campus.[11]

There are advantages and disadvantages in using police or other law officials in school media centers. Their mere presence may do much to prevent theft and disorder, although this is very difficult to evaluate. The fact that they are in uniform lends a feeling of security to the media center environment. The image they reflect should be safety, concern, and courtesy. Police persons give undivided attention to suspicious moves by would-be thieves or mischief makers, whereas library staff members, attempting to "police" while performing other duties, have constant distractions. Police personnel can also give advice on security precautions, fire protection measures, door locks, exterior lighting, door alarms, and other measures of protection.

11. Alan Jay Lincoln and Carol Zall Lincoln, "The Impact of Crime in Public Libraries," *Library & Archival Security* 3:134 (Fall/Winter 1980).

On the other hand, there are likely corollary disadvantages to the use of police in school media centers. The presence of a law officer may give the impression that no library user is to be trusted, and this could be a strain on the rapport between patrons and staff. The atmosphere may seem restricted and appear to be more like a prison than a library.

The problems of security faced by media specialists should be shared by the entire school population. Administrators, teachers, counselors, and media specialists need to work together to develop schoolwide plans to reduce security threats within and outside the media center. In large school systems, such as Seattle Public Schools, where there is a district-level chief of security, plans for security control of media centers are coordinated and directed through this office.

Specific instructions should be prepared for dealing with tornados, hurricanes, and fires. Orientation sessions and practice drills should be a vital part of the overall plan. Members of the community, such as fire-fighters and police, can assist with planning and serve as resource persons: assembly speakers, in-service lecturers, etc.

An active, uniformly enforced visitor-control system should be in operation in the school. Posted signs, advising visitors to sign in at the office, would be part of the plan, and visitor permits would be issued. All teachers should assist (when possible) by introducing themselves to visitors in hallways. By offering directional assistance, they could also help screen out undesirables. Media specialists, by asking all strangers who enter the media center to present their visitor passes, could help identify vagrants, dope pushers, child molesters, and other potentially harmful individuals.

A schoolwide policy pertaining to students who transfer and withdraw from school is another important precaution that can prevent collection erosion. The transferal form should have a slot for library clearance that requires the signature of a member of the media center staff. Cooperation is needed between the office personnel and the media center to stop unnecessary losses to the collection through this frequent and silent form of theft.

Often the media center's line of communication is via the home room or first-period teacher. Messages, overdue notices, and announcements would not meet their destinations without the assistance of these teachers. It is exceptionally helpful when teachers jog students' memories in regard to their obligations to the media center.

Teachers can alleviate some of the problems of nonreturned materials, discipline in the library, and mistreatment of library resources. They can also help prevent unauthorized removal of items from the media center. The media specialist blesses those elementary-grade teachers who stand at the door as their classes leave the center, checking to see that all books were checked out properly.

Teachers can help also by giving realistic assignments to their students. Outside work assigned *en masse,* without regard to the ratio of media resources to class sizes, can tempt frantic students to steal. They may slip materials out of the media center, or hide scarce items in the center, so they will not be required to share with other students.

Student organizations can also aid the media center in its drive to mend security leaks. For example, student councils often conduct campaigns to fight the problems of theft and nonreturn of materials in addition to the monetary contributions they make toward the purchase and replacement of books taken from shelves. Posters, articles in the school paper, announcements over the intercom and schoolwide contests for ferreting out lost materials are a few methods student councils and other students might use to stimulate the consciences of their peers.

The media specialist alone cannot halt the shrinking of the collection and the deterioration of services that result from media center abuse. In view of the spiraling costs of media; limited budgets, eroded by inflation; increased demands on education; and the pressures of meeting state and regional standards, the task is Herculean but not hopeless. All members of a school are needed on the security team. Security begins with people, not equipment and devices. Administrators, teachers, students, support personnel, and media staff need to plot and plan together to lessen the dangers and reduce costs of security breaches.

University Libraries

University libraries and their resources represent the accumulation of the world's knowledge. Some of the greatest literary treasures of mankind are available in university research collections. These scholarly libraries have two main purposes: to make materials available for patrons' use and to preserve materials. Yet, ironically, university libraries are forced to take action to protect their resources against the very people they exist to serve. Books must be *protected* from people. Careless abuse, theft, deliberate mutilation, vandalism, faulty processing, and conservation ignorance deplete the nation's academic collections.

Headlines in the media, as well as in professional and book-trade publications, have spotlighted the dramatic rise in crimes directed toward university and other types of libraries. In the last ten years, articles on library theft and vandalism have become more visible, and entries in *Library Literature,* under the headings "Thefts and Losses of Books,

Periodicals, etc." and "Library Protection Systems," have grown longer, accordingly. Another evidence of rising concern with library security was seen in 1975, when a new and needed journal, *Library Security Newsletter* (later changed to *Library and Archival Security*), emerged on the scene. In the last decade, several new methods have been introduced to retrieve valuable materials that have been pilfered and to reduce theft attempts. Since 1976, a list of lost/stolen manuscripts has appeared regularly in the Society of American Archivists' Security Register. *A B Bookman's Weekly* instituted a "Missing Books" section in 1977. *Library Journal* intermittently includes a timely column, "Security in Libraries." In early 1982 a new automation breakthrough to reduce biblioklepto-mania was announced. BAM-BAM (Bookline Alert Missing Books and Manuscripts), a computer network, was implemented by the Antiquarian Booksellers' Association of America. It operates through international interlibrary connections in the United States, Canada, and Europe, making information pertaining to stolen or missing books available.

Due to the nature of their collections, university libraries are particularly vulnerable to the professional thief. One widely publicized example of their heinous library crime is the James Shinn case. Shinn, who uses other aliases, was an expert on rare books, and as a connoisseur he selected only the best titles as he traveled from state to state, from library to library. He left a trail at over a dozen academic libraries across the nation, until he was apprehended in Oberlin, Ohio, after attempting to rob the Oberlin College Library in April 1981. Shinn jumped bail. When he struck again, months later in Allentown, Pennsylvania, he was detected by an alert library staff at Muhlenberg College, and the FBI closed in and arrested him. Late in 1982 he was sentenced by a federal judge to two consecutive ten-year terms. Other charges against Shinn are still pending. He may be responsible for stealing up to $500,000 worth of books, mostly eighteenth- and nineteenth-century publications.[12]

The Shinn episode is not an isolated case. Robert Kindred, another traveling book thief, who specialized in full-color plates, was arrested in 1982 when he was caught in the act of robbing the University of Illinois Library at Champaign-Urbana. Previously, he had razored $100,000 worth of prints from books at Rice University (Houston) and $38,000 worth of plates belonging to Texas A & M University Library.[13] Even

12. "Security in Libraries: Professional Book Thief Nailed in Oberlin, Ohio," *Library Journal* 106:1267 (15 June 1981). "In the News: Librarians Trigger Recapture of Book-Theft Suspect Shinn," *American Libraries* 13:110 (Feb. 1982). "Security in Libraries: Shinn Gets Maximum Sentence for Book Theft: 20 Years," *Library Journal* 107:2210 (1 Dec. 1982).

13. "Security in Libraries: Following Theft, Rice University Will Sell Recovered Prints," *Library Journal* 107:2212 (1 Dec. 1982).

earlier, Harvard University's Museum of Comparative Zoology lost over $500,000 worth of priceless, rare editions of scientific and artistic value, including works by John W. Audubon, Louis Agassiz, and others.[14]

Several particularly abhorrent examples of university-library plunder are successful raids by brazen thieves who posed as officials of a new microfilm company and removed sets of periodicals on the pretext of microfilming them.[15]

A "first" in the annals of academic library theft occurred in 1979, when a library publication announced the theft of an OCLC terminal. The $3,700 terminal was stolen from the Library Department of the City College of New York.[16] The following year, Illinois Benedictine College at Lisle reported the loss of an OCLC terminal that was stolen from a locked technical processing room.[17]

Not all academic library larceny can be attributed to the professional and selective thief. Staff members, janitors, and of course students are responsible for a large measure of collection attrition. A study by Weiss, based on a questionnaire completed by students at a large urban university to determine why students steal and mutilate materials, reached a surprising conclusion. The survey showed that it was the student with a good academic standing who committed acts of library abuse. The author hypothesized that the students' behavior reflects academic pressures.[18] Matt T. Roberts offered this same theory more than ten years earlier.[19]

Mutilation of library books and periodicals is an egregious act that plagues the academic library, and several surveys have studied the extent and probable causes of this accelerating, wanton destruction. A national survey by Hendrick and Murfin, in 1972, found that the problem of periodical mutilation was widespread and was experienced in almost all college and university libraries.[20]

Gouke and Murfin, who call periodical mutilation "the insidious dis-

14. "Security in Libraries: Harvard Zoology Library Counts Rare Books Lost," *Library Journal* 106:1874 (1 Oct. 1981).

15. J. Wayne Baker, "Perspiring Periodicals Thief," *American Libraries* 3:228 (March 1972).

16. Slade Richard Gandert, "Protecting Your Collection," *Library & Archival Security* 4:108 (1982).

17. "Security in Libraries: Pros Snatch OCLC Terminal from Illinois Benedictine," *Library Journal* 105:2537 (15 Dec. 1980).

18. Dana Weiss, "Book Theft and Book Mutilation in a Large Urban University Library," *College & Research Libraries* 42:345 (July 1981).

19. Matt T. Roberts, "Guards, Turnstiles, Electronic Devices, and the Illusion of Security," *College & Research Libraries* 29:259–75 (July 1968).

20. Clyde Hendrick and Marjorie Murfin, "Project Library Ripoff: A Study of Periodical Mutilation in a University Library," *College & Research Libraries* 35:402–11 (Nov. 1974).

ease," made a study of magazine damage in a large academic library as a follow-up to a 1973 survey. The authors documented the extent of periodical mutilation and viewed the effects of a public relations program launched three years previously. They also assessed the effects of a "gate security" system that was installed about four years earlier. They found that both the gate security and the public relations appeared to achieve a reduction of mutilation. Their study also supported the theory that damage breeds damage.[21]

The University of Nebraska Library reported recently that, in one year's time, over 1,100 pages from magazines had to be replaced and 672 complete issues had to be ordered to substitute for periodicals that had been stolen or severely damaged.[22]

The provision of copy machines does not seem to mitigate this destruction. The use of coin-operated copiers is usually accompanied by queuing situations. Whether caused by shortage of equipment or temporarily malfunctioning machines, the results are often the same: disgruntled and frustrated patrons who are likely to mutilate library resources.

David Taylor, in a reprint article in *College and Research Libraries News,* called attention not only to the usual razor-and-scissors damage to library materials, but mentioned another growing problem: marking and underlining in books. Yellow and other pastel "hi-liners" used liberally on pages of print, are annoying and distracting to other readers. They destroy thought patterns and are another form of mutilation.[23]

Some university libraries have fought back by mounting exhibits to draw attention to the senseless but costly defacement of library materials. Displays of disfigured periodicals, gutted volumes, books with covers ripped off, and mutilated illustrations are placed in glass cases on public view, as victims of wanton library crime and mute witnesses to needless destruction of intellectual materials. A library in England, wishing to make a stronger visual impact, borrowed confiscated weapons from the local police station and placed them (knives, razors, lead belts, and darts) alongside the "tortured" books.[24]

University libraries suffer extensively from vandalism, a reprehensible crime that exists in many forms and varieties. The Undergraduate Library of the University of North Carolina has experienced disappearing stack

21. M. N. Gouke and Marjorie Murfin, "Periodical Mutilation: The Insidious Disease," *Library Journal* 105:1795–97 (15 Sept. 1980).

22. "Security in Libraries: University of Nebraska Reports Sharp Rise in Mutilation," *Library Journal* 107:2212 (1 Dec. 1982).

23. David Taylor, "Enemies of Books," *College & Research Libraries News* 12:318 (Oct. 1981).

24. "Milder Enemies," *Library Association Record* 81:288 (June 1979).

signs (which are thought to be adorning the walls of dormitory rooms). Another library has problems keeping microfiche viewers in repair: the glass plates seem to disappear into thin air. In restrooms all across the country, graffiti pops up overnight like mushrooms. A state university in Texas experienced a racial graffiti feud that lasted more than six weeks when a student wrote filthy and insulting remarks on the restroom walls, targeted at a library janitor of another ethnic group. Custodial efforts to remove the inscriptions only increased their frequency and vitriol. After warning the custodian that he would have the last word, the "artist" carved insults into a marble panel in the men's restroom. After the chiseled words were obliterated with a sealing compound, the entire panel was pulled from the wall and left on the floor, broken into several segments.[25]

Some time ago, entire drawers were stolen from the card catalog at the University of Illinois Library; the thief was never detected nor the motivation behind the action understood. Without doubt the saddest memory of most university librarians is the "student activism" in the '60s, when library vandalism was at an all-time high.

In 1981, when Princeton University announced the termination of Firestone Memorial Library's unlimited access policy (after 33 years), effective the following year, one of the stated reasons was vandalism. This rationale was linked with other problems, such as theft, mutilation, and shortage of space.[26]

In addition to people, other enemies wreak damage on university libraries. Some of the most frequent nonhuman hazards include fires, storms, floods, vermin, mold, extremes of temperature and humidity, light, sunshine, dust, and air pollution. Steps must be taken by library administrators to prevent each of these threats from becoming a reality.

There is rising concern over the problems of library damage perpetrated by both human and nonhuman forces. At last, concern is replacing complacency. No longer are the alert accused of being alarmists. Library administrators are seeking solutions for their particular security needs. Attempts to circumvent security weaknesses are being aided with both inside and outside protective measures.

Inside Security Protection. Some college and university libraries attempt to halt theft and accidental removal of library materials through the provision of exit guards, posted at egress points as checkers or inspectors. There may also be a turnstile to improve traffic control at these

25. Interview with Charles Lee Dwyer, Curator, Thomason Room, Sam Houston State University Library, Huntsville, Texas, 21 Jan. 1983.
26. "Security Problems Prod Princeton to Impose Access Curbs." *Library Journal* 106:2171 (15 Nov. 1981).

exit stations. Building-design features, such as corridors or mounted barriers, may channel patrons into queues. This method, of course, is far from new, and was widely used before the invention of electronic security systems. A 1967 survey indicated that nearly 50 percent of academic libraries used the turnstile/guard method at that time.[27] The combination of turnstile and guard (or guards alone) is still used in many university libraries.

Checking is not identical in all libraries that utilize an exit guard. The procedure in many instances extends only to examination of the books in hand. Other institutions require thorough searches, including purses, briefcases, backpacks, and all packages. Signs at both the entrance and exit forewarn patrons of this inspection. An apparent weakness in this theft-prevention method is the ease with which patrons can conceal materials on their person. Interior pockets on coats or shirts, even boots, can be used by the smuggler. Inspections do not resort to "frisking." Another problem with the guarded exit is the fact that there are always alternative escape routes: delivery doors, unwelded windows, fire escapes, etc.

However, the variable that most often determines the success or failure of the exit-guard method is the skill of the person employed as inspector. These attendants may be students, either graduate or undergraduate; library support personnel, assigned on a part-time basis; or individuals hired by the library for the sole purpose of providing this service. Workers on the library payroll are usually trained and directed by the library, in contrast to contract guard services.

There seems to be a decided preference to employ older, retired persons as guards. Student help has often proved inadequate for this demanding task. It is difficult for many students to deal with problem patrons, who protest and resist the checking procedure or attempt to remove materials illegitimately. Student workers are often hesitant to inspect the belongings of faculty members or older graduate students, and the inflexibility of their class schedules may place limitations on their availability to the library. It is interesting to note that one survey found female students are more effective than males as exit checkers.[28]

Protection by guards at the point of exit will not be sufficient for large academic libraries. Closed-stack areas often require monitors who issue passes and check possessions upon exit. Reserve rooms may be controlled by attendants who enforce the policy of surrendering personal items before patrons enter the room. Rare-book divisions usually employ

27. "Security Survey Indicates Turnstiles Widely Used," *Library Journal* 92:3362 (1 Oct. 1967).
28. Ibid., p. 3364.

guard/receptionists during library hours. Attendants may be needed to move about the building, maintaining order, observing patrons' activities, and surveying areas of the library that are blind spots for the staff and are likely to be trouble zones, such as stacks, reading rooms, and alcoves.

Advantages and disadvantages may accrue through the use of library staff as security attendants. In contrast to contract guards, they are already familiar with most library procedures, aware of "building use only" items, and more likely to detect efforts and schemes to get these through the door (such as attaching false pockets in reference materials and taping over the use-restriction identification).

Staff members may be recognizable to the library patrons and may be received with more cooperation and responsiveness by those who are inspected. Library directors often feel more in control of the guard service when attendants are on the library payroll. It is simpler to rearrange schedules and shift positions if an inspector does not prove satisfactory. Shorter time spans by in-house guards are not only easy to assign, but often prove to be advantageous. Guard duty can become boring and tedious after prolonged hours, causing a decline in effectiveness. Frequent alternation of guards could assure less boredom and more alertness. Also, if a library utilizes guard service only at specific or peak times of the day, or certain periods of the academic year, it may be easier for the library director to handle short-term needs internally. After a careful analysis of comparative costs, it may be determined that in-house security protection is also less costly to the library than contract guards service.

There are disadvantages in library-staff assignment for security duties. Many library workers may intensely dislike being cast as a guard, lack self-confidence and feel inadequate to handling problem situations. Even after receiving on-the-job training, they may feel that they lack sufficient preparation. It may be hard for them to concentrate completely on the security work at hand, especially if they alternate between guard work and other duties. Their primary functions, on the other hand, may suffer in weaker operations elsewhere in the library.

It may be tempting to assign in-house guards other tasks to perform during lulls at the exit gate, but this mix of duties may be detrimental to security. Not only can other activities be distracting, but the impression and impact of having a guard on duty can be nullified.

A growing number of university libraries are turning to electronic theft-prevention devices to protect their resources. These systems, first introduced in the mid-'60s, all operate to detect materials improperly charged. A signal sounds when a patron with such items passes a sensing screen. Most screens are strategically placed, by the circulation desk, so that all materials leaving the library must have their detector tags desensitized (during the circulation process) to prevent triggering an alarm. Should an alarm go off, the circulation assistant must respond. In a sense, the circulation worker serves as a guard.

None of the systems on the market is 100 percent effective; however, library administrators who use them claim loss reduction of 70 to 95 percent.[29]

Outside Security Protection. Many university libraries seek solutions to security problems through outside assistance. For example, campus police are utilized. In some instances, security police are on duty within the library from opening to closing. Some security systems require only periodic checks by a campus police person, once an hour or less frequently. Other libraries have police only during night hours. A frequent practice is to use security patrols at night, offering not only in-building protection but escort service from the library to the parking lot or campus dormitories. Many universities utilize volunteer groups to assist campus police with escort services. Members of fraternity houses and various university organizations often serve as safety patrols. Young men escort female colleagues, individually or in groups, as they go to and from their dormitories and campus libraries.

Campus police often report to the library to assist with the transfer of money to the university cashier or to vaults. It is also common for police to help close and lock the library at the conclusion of night hours. Some university libraries call for additional campus police coverage during examination periods, which is a time of tension for many students—a period amenable to theft and vandalism. Frequently, academic libraries take steps to ameliorate the rapport with students during this stressful time by lengthening library hours. A library on a Texas campus serves free coffee to "night owls," cramming for finals, from 11:00 p.m. to closing time at 2:00 a.m.

Emergency telephones can facilitate campus police surveillance. These phones can be established in various spots, on campus grounds and in buildings. This type of "hotline" requires no breakage of glass, no dialing. Lifting the receiver alerts the campus police to a need for help at the location of the phone. Before a word is uttered, a police car is heading in that direction.

Such telephone systems in library buildings can be immeasurably effective. One library that utilizes the emergency telephone system is the University of Wisconsin's Madison Memorial Library. Since this library is a state resource, it is open to all citizens of Wisconsin. Many nonuni-

29. Bahr, *Book Theft,* p. 111.

versity people enter its doors, including an occasional "street person." Library patrons and staff, when faced with harassment, exposure, and other problems, can be in direct contact with the campus-police switch-board by lifting the emergency phone off its hook. The mere presence of these phones and the signs explaining their use can be a deterrent to violations of personal and building safety.[30]

Another solution to the library security problem may be contract security guards. Through arrangements with a professional guard service, a library can bolster its protection by providing additional sets of eyes and ears. Contract guards' major roles are to prevent security violations, detect potential threats, and report breaks in library policies. Guard service is a supplement to police protection, not a replacement; the two roles are not identical. Contract guards can act as police witnesses and make a citizen's arrest; however, their knowledge of the law need not be as extensive as that of police. Primarily, police personnel enforce laws and regulations and often are not involved in security matters, until a violation has occurred, whereas a security guard's major task is to *prevent* infractions of the law. The aim is not to catch the lawbreaker so much as to place a damper on law breaking. Admittedly, there is an overlap in surveillance when police personnel are assigned to library buildings to perform guard duties.

Many firms today supply contract guards and there is much competition in the field. Some of these businesses are long-established, professional services, such as Burns International Security Services and Pinkerton's. However, there are also many high-risk "rent-a-cop" firms. Libraries and universities should consider many factors before selecting a guard service. The low bid should not be the sole basis for the decision. According to security consultant Charles Schnabolk of Bellaire Associates, New York, three additional considerations should be the training the guards receive, the company's reputation, and the quality and caliber of the guards.[31]

Points to check during the selection process are as follows:

1. Are the guards bonded? Are they licensed?
2. Does the firm conduct a background check on its employees? (Some consultants recommend fingerprint checks.)
3. What percentage of the fee is paid to the guard? (The rationale is that better-paid guards provide better service.)

30. J. A. Tuttle, "Security and Safety: University of Wisconsin Madison Memorial Library Steps to Solve Problems," *Wisconsin Library Bulletin* 76:136 (May–June 1980).

31. "Security: Guard Services, Closing Contract Loopholes," *Nation's Schools & Colleges* 1:26 (Nov. 1974).

4. If the guard is "moonlighting," what is his or her total workload per week? (A walking zombie might be the result if weekly hours exceed 65.)
5. What is the educational level of the guards?
6. Who controls the criteria for the selection of guards: the firm or the institution? (There are mixed opinions on this.)
7. What supervision of its guards is provided by the firm?
8. How extensive is the training supplied by the security service?

Libraries that hire guard services differ in their assignment of duties. In many cases, the guard will be stationary and will "man" the library exit, checking for unauthorized removal of materials. Depending upon the size of the building, the number of users, and the need for security, one guard—or an additional one—may function at the entrance, observing the persons admitted and perhaps requesting identification. Other guards may be needed to patrol the building. These individuals may have dual functions: providing information as well as seeking to deter theft, vandalism, and other problems.

The newly hired security guard should have a thorough orientation to the library. Although the guard may be highly trained in industrial security, he or she may have little knowledge of the special problems that confront university libraries and archival collections. The in-service session should be complete, providing a walk-through tour, detailed floor plans, copies of the library policies, and an explanation of his or her role in regard to library staff and administration. The guard also needs to know, say, campus-wide security measures: contingency plans for fires, storms, student riots, etc. A strong relationship between the guard and the campus police is most desirable. Roles should be clearly identified, as well as cooperative activities. Orientation should include on-the-job training with the campus security division.

A detailed job description for the library guard is essential. Also, a list of specific duties is necessary. These documents, of course, will vary with each library, according to its security needs. Pat Schindler identified a number of functions that a security guard can be expected to provide:

1. Access Control
2. Control of Removal of Items
3. Fire Watch
4. Crowd Control
5. Information and Assistance
6. Inspection of Safety and Fire Fighting Equipment
7. Control of Fire Evacuation
8. Observation of Employee Activity
9. Patrol of Premises

10. Parking Lot Control
11. Lock Up
12. Setting and Testing of Alarm Systems
13. Building Evacuation during Emergencies Such as Bomb Threats
14. Observation
15. Reports Covering Observations in All Phases of Operations[32]

Security guards who are selected for library service should be individuals who command respect from both patrons and staff. It is mandatory that their appearance, demeanor, dress, and personality be above reproach. The ability to be calm and courteous while dealing with troublesome patrons is a prerequisite. The successful guard projects an image of self-confidence, but not bravado; exercises vigilance without intimidation. Friendliness, accompanied by firmness, is a necessary trait, whereas patronizing and threatening stances can destroy the guard's effectiveness.

Library administrators should exercise caution in assigning nonsecurity duties to guards. The image reflected by guards may be one of the most important deterrents to security problems; however, it is fragile. Placing security personnel in demeaning positions may shatter their positive image. Schindler lists four duties that should *not* be assigned to guards:

1. Janitorial Duties
2. Book Shelving
3. Disciplining Employees Violating Rules
4. Demeaning Duties that Lower Esteem of the Guards [*sic*] Image in the Eyes of Employees and Visitors[33]

Are there advantages to be gained through employment of contract rather than in-house guards? There are several that can be identified. The preservice training that contract guards receive must be considered a strong advantage. Most states require a training period for licensing security guards. The length of time, curriculum, and levels of training vary from state to state. Guards hired for library security may not only be trained, but may be seasoned by years of experience as well. Some may have specialized skills in such areas as emergency first-aid, crowd management, fire prevention and control, etc.

Contract guards, due to their affiliation with a commercial security firm, are covered by liability protection. Their company assumes responsibility for its employees' actions, providing insurance to cover the firm

32. Pat Schindler, "The Use of Security Guards in Libraries," *Library Security Newsletter* 2:3 (Summer 1978).
33. Ibid.

and the library in the event of charges of negligence, false arrest, mistakes by the guard, and accusations. This type of insurance coverage is a real bonus to the library.

If contract guards perform poorly, it is easy to have them removed and replaced, and less personal and traumatic than removing in-house security personnel. In the library, the in-house guard is likely to be at the bottom of the "pecking order," with little hope of ascending the career ladder. There may be more opportunities for advancement within the security firm. Also, the contract guard may enjoy more fringe benefits, such as money for uniforms, liability insurance, and payment for telephone calls—in addition to the usual sick leave, vacation, and social security. Thus the morale of the contract guard may be higher; he or she may be more concerned with career growth and, as a result, perform better on the job.

The aura or image of the contract guard may be more convincing than that of the "inside" security guard. Self-confidence on the part of the security person may be transferred to library patrons, making them feel safe and secure.

Opinions are mixed in regard to the dress code for library guards, either in-house or "outside." A uniform identifies the employee immediately as a security person. When threats to safety and security arise, it is easy for patrons to recognize and locate the guard(s) on duty and solicit help. The uniform creates a certain image of authority and may provide a psychological deterrent to crime. Undesirables may terminate their library visits when they encounter a uniformed attendant. However, the philosophy of many libraries is that their security guards maintain a low profile and convey helpfulness and courtesy rather than an image of policelike authority.

Some individuals feel that college and university students are alienated by "authority uniforms." To overcome such negative aspects, a number of libraries insist that their plainclothes personnel wear blazers with security identification or lapel patches. This gives a less threatening or challenging impression and casts the guards into roles as assistants who supply information and directions, rather than that of stormtroopers.

Guards should not be armed, except in extreme cases; and then, only if the security person has received special training with firearms. In high-risk situations, a nightstick can carry a great deal of authority.

Some university libraries utilize uniformed guards only for night hours, when security threats are more likely. Rice University (Houston), for example, is open until 1:00 a.m. each morning. A uniformed guard (usually an unarmed student, trained by campus police) provides surveillance within the library during night hours. This is in addition to the usual entrance/exit guard and the campus-police patrol in the area surrounding the library.[34]

In-house and "outside" security protection guards, as a rule, are assisted in their duties by technical aids. These differ, of course, from campus to campus. Exits, other than the main one, are often wired with fire-alarm buzzers. Intercom systems, to page security guards, are available in many libraries. Walkie-talkies and pagers are a boon to nonstationary guards. Many urban-campus libraries have "panic buttons" at strategic places in stacks and other locations where users might need help. The silent alarm button is particularly appropriate to signal for assistance. Another often-used security measure is a direct telephone hookup with the campus security office. Closed-circuit television cameras and microphones provide sophisticated surveillance; however, not all libraries can afford this expensive form of protection.

The University of Wisconsin–Madison has established a "whistle-stop" program. Patrons can check out a whistle at the circulation desk (or bring their own) and, in the event of harassment, can blow their whistles for help, either for themselves or someone else. Patrons are advised, through a signage system, to call for help loudly and to report all incidents to the circulation counter.[35]

All university library employees should be sensitive to security threats. Even though not assigned to specific positions of security, most staff members constantly face decision-making situations that pertain to security. Library policies and procedures for dealing with various types of security problems should be spelled out in staff handbooks. Staff positions, at all levels, should have input into designing the procedures for dealing with each type of infringement. The University of Wisconsin–Platteville has a manual that covers fires, bomb threats, medical emergencies, student disturbances, tornado warnings, emergency operations, etc.[36]

On many campuses an overall, university-wide plan is established by the security division. Coordinators in each building, including the library, are appointed. Training sessions are held (through the security office) to prepare all university employees to handle security programs. This includes hands-on use of emergency equipment, such as fire extinguishers, alarm signals, etc. Publications pertaining to safety and security are widely distributed.

Protection for academic libraries is ongoing and it concerns everyone.

34. Interview with Samuel M. Carrington, director, Fondren Library, Rice University, Houston, Texas, 6 Jan. 1983.

35. Tuttle, "Security and Safety," p. 136.

36. "Security Systems in Use," p. 134.

Regardless of the methods used to protect patrons, collections, and buildings, constant monitoring is needed. Evaluations should be continuous.

Public Libraries

The American public library has long been characterized by its open-door policy and its accessibility. It was established to provide services to *all* members of the community. This admirable philosophy, noble as it is, places the public library in a particularly vulnerable position. Serious and recreational readers, research students, business people, community leaders, and children of all ages pour through its doors; but across the same thresholds pass prostitutes, mendicants, child molesters, winos, bibliokleptomaniacs, exhibitionists, vagrants, pickpockets, drug dealers, and other miscreants. Certainly the democratic concept of the public's right to free access to the library is fraught with probelms. Although the public library faces many of the same security infractions experienced by university and school libraries, it seems to attract more than its share of aberrant individuals. Furthermore, its patrons are not subject to background checks, as are possible through grades records and transcripts, and there are no withdrawal procedures when patrons move.

The public library administrator often faces a paradox: Which should have priority, the open-door service ethic or enforcement of security and safety measures? When the door of the urban library is wide open, there will always be disruptive and problem patrons. When "bag people" come into libraries for refuge and sex perverts for exploitation, the serious library patron may be frightened away. No reader feels safe rubbing elbows with tramps and pickpockets. Some libraries warn their clientele by posting signs in the reading rooms, alerting them to watch their billfolds and purses. Restrooms and secluded stacks can become the territory of the sexual deviant, causing a threat to the other patrons. To provide restroom safety (and to prevent vandalism), many libraries have resorted to locked doors. (The key may be checked out at the circulation desk.) Some libraries are installing special locks on restroom doors that open only when a specially designed token is slipped into a slot. Another safety device is the "potty pull"—an overhead chain (in each stall) that can be yanked as a signal for help. It acts as a silent alarm, alerting the circulation desk or the security guard.

Noisy school children and young adults often rupture the quiet atmosphere of public libraries, causing staff dismay and patron anger. While their behavior is usually noncriminal, it can be a serious problem, especially during after-school hours. The noise and nuisance can drive patrons away. Also, pranks can get out of hand and become dangerous, requiring close staff monitoring. A rearrangement of staff schedules may help. Workers who are skillful in handling children and teenagers should be assigned duty for the after-school hours. The library could also follow a suggestion by the director of security at Brooklyn Public Library, Frank DeRosa, who advocates selective enforcement of a policy that requires youngsters with records of previous disturbances to show a valid library card before being admitted to the library.[37]

One needs only to peruse recent library literature to understand the magnitude and range of the security problems confronting many public libraries. The following accounts are a sample of security violations in the past five years.

A statewide survey of library crime in public libraries in New Hampshire revealed that intentional book damage was the most common disruption, reported by 43 percent of the respondents. Verbal abuse of staff was next highest, indicated by 27 percent of the respondents. A random sample among 100 Massachusetts libraries of library security problems showed that 80 percent of the responding libraries experienced intentional book damage and vandalism, outside and inside the building. Damage to patrons' and staffs' cars was reported at 31 and 40 percent respectively. Over 59 percent reported verbal abuse to staff and 17 percent indicated assault against patrons.[38]

Tucson Public Library System (Arizona) several years ago initiated a CLSI bar-coding project. This was not only a boon to circulation, it also helped libraries inventory their resources more accurately. One branch discovered book losses totalling 17 percent of its collection. Another reported a similar book loss. At both libraries, nonprint materials suffered a higher percentage of loss: 64 percent of one collection and 52 percent of the other branch's holdings.[39]

On October 2, 1980, a San Diego public library was torched by arsonists, for a loss of $150,000 in structural damages and $250,000 in content damages. Vandals had broken out a window to set the fire in a workroom.[40] A library fire in Rolla, Missouri, caused $900,000 in damages. This rural library, which was hit by an arsonist, had no alarm system. It *did* have an oversupply of false security.[41]

37. Frank J. DeRosa, "The Disruptive Patron," *Library & Archival Security* 3:36 (Fall–Winter 1980).

38. Lincoln and Lincoln, "The Impact of Crime in Public Libraries," pp. 128–29.

39. "Security in Libraries: Stolen Books & Overdues: New Security Tactics Tried," *Library Journal* 104:878 (15 April 1979).

40. "Security in Libraries: San Diego Branch Library Torched by Arsonists," *Library Journal* 105:2537 (15 Dec. 1980).

41. "Security in Libraries: Fire in Rolla, Missouri," *Library Journal* 107:2212 (1 Dec. 1982).

Putnam Valley Library (New York), just before its 1981 National Library Week, was the target of extensive vandalism which resulted in cancellation of many of its week-long activities. The malicious damages read like a horror tale:

> Catalog and borrower file cards were strewn throughout the wing of the new building; copy machine ink was smeared on carpeting in three rooms, and a slide projector, carousel, and classical tapes were destroyed. Also: a fire had been started in a sink, thermostat wires were snipped, and the oil burner dismantled. Working on the outside, vandals tore open a ventilating unit and ripped off a light fixture.[42]

Although not endemic in public libraries, the problem of delinquent borrowers is persistent. Theft through nonreturn of materials is frequent. False identity, incorrect addresses, and illegitimate use of borrowers' cards compound the problem. Various methods of attacking this rising concern are being tried across the country. Some public libraries use the "soft" approach: they have abolished fines alltogether or they have periodic amnesty weeks or months. Campaigns are launched through posters and the local radio and press to appeal to the public's conscience, urging materials be returned. Raffles and awards have been instituted, with giveaways to those with "clear" records. Prizes range from hamburgers to paperbacks.

Other public libraries have moved in the opposite direction, adopting "get tough" policies. More and more specialized collections have been placed on closed reserve. Policies have been amended in regard to borrowers' cards, reducing the length of time between renewals. A few libraries have established rules requiring deposits on materials when checked out and refunding the money on their return. Others are adopting such tactics as sending Mailgrams, or hiring collectors, or using the threat of legal action. (In 1979, a Colorado man was sent to jail for 90 days for failure to pay for 45 library books that he did not return.)[43]

The problems of nonreturn of materials, the disruptive patron, book damage, vandalism, arson, and other serious violations are being met by public libraries through both "inside" and "outside" security measures.

Inside Security Protection. Public libraries have developed and are implementing security procedures through cooperation with their boards, administration, and staff members. They are receiving both sympathy

42. "Security in Libraries: Vandalism Snuffs Out NLW Plans for Putnam Valley, New York," *Library Journal* 106:1269 (15 June 1981). Reprinted from *Library Journal*, published by R. R. Bowker Co. (a Xerox Company). Copyright © 1981 by Xerox Corporation.

43. *Houston Chronicle*, 5 Feb. 1979.

and action from local and state governments in the form of city and county ordinances and state legislation. In addition to governmental support, public libraries, just as their academic counterparts, are utilizing technology and a variety of personnel patterns.

There are differences and similarities in the efforts of university and public libraries vis-à-vis security protection. The large public libraries often use in-house personnel for guard attendants, monitoring entrances and exits and patrolling troublesome areas. Some of the largest have a director of security on their staffs. Brooklyn, Queensborough, and New York City public libraries are prime examples of this practice. "Senior Investigator (Bibliographic)" is the term used for New York Public Library's head security officers who supervise the "library attendant guards" on duty in the five-story central building. The senior investigators are on 24-hour emergency call. Attendants were first installed in the New York Public Library's reading room in 1901. Today, guards check each person upon entrance to the two main reading rooms. At the two exits, patrons' possessions are carefully examined by uniformed guards.[44]

Brooklyn Public Library's security chief has introduced color-coded badges for his employees, each color designating specific areas accessible to the wearer. Other libraries have had unpleasant results from using personalized staff badges. Although they (the badges) provide instant identification to patrons who need information and assistance, they also furnish opportunities for misuse. (Library employees who work in both public and nonpublic areas of libraries have been plagued by obscene telephone calls after name tags were required.)

Secret code words are also used by library staffs, as a quick, unobtrusive way to alert each other to potential dangers.

Delinquent borrowers are the bane of most libraries, as mentioned earlier. Schools and universities have a few more resources that can be used to assure the return of materials; however, academic libraries complain about nonreturn of books by graduating students. Some public libraries are using in-house personnel to help alleviate this type of collection erosion. Knoxville–Knox County Public Library, in Tennessee, made news by hiring a part-time employee as a collector as early as 1976. The library sends a Mailgram first. If the materials are not returned, the collector makes a personal visit. Statistics attest to the success of these unique house calls: in one year, more than 1,700 items were recovered, valued at over $12,000.[45]

The large public libraries are turning to technology to solve their

44. Gandert, "Protecting Your Collection," p. 94.
45. Nancy H. Petersen, "Upping the Ante on Overdues," *Library & Archival Security* 3:26 (Spring 1980).

severe problems of theft, arson, and vandalism. Recent advances, utilizing ultrasonic detectors, furnish greater protection against building intrusion. Security hardware, in this age of the transistor and the laser, is more compact, requires less maintenance, and is proving to be more durable. These sophisticated (and efficacious) inventions not only activate alarm systems, they phone for help through automatic multichannel dialers. They can also trigger signs that flash on the library's exterior.

Many public libraries are also utilizing electronic security systems to detect improperly checked-out materials. These monitoring devices are improving library services and are reducing collection attrition. For example, when the Houston Public Library experienced heavy theft from its downtown Central Library in the late 1970s, the system director posted guards at the doors. Later, in 1979, when losses reached a total of $73,400 in one year, an electronic detection system was installed.[46] Jay B. Clark, chief of technical services, attributes the system with a significant reduction in theft. Two of the larger branch libraries are now equipped with electronic systems. The decision has been made, based on their success, to install similar devices in future branches.[47]

Outside Security Protection. Although public libraries face many security problems, their allies among municipal and county governments offer protection: city police and county sheriff departments, for example. They also have access to such agencies as physical and mental health clinics, social service agencies, and county departments. Through cooperative arrangements, the public library can utilize referral procedures, staff counseling, assistance with problem patrons, and a variety of other services.

A large urban library and its inner-city branches may have city police personnel on duty continuously during open hours. However, since municipal police forces are frequently undermanned, the library may be served by partial police protection or surveillance from a distance. In these days of economic austerity, some libraries, formerly staffed with city police, are forced to seek protection elsewhere. Boston Public Library, for instance, during pre-Proposition 2½ days, utilized city police for security patrol. When money shortage forced the city to redeploy its police force, the officers were removed from the library and assigned elsewhere. Boston Public Library then hired Pinkerton guards to prevent crime from taking over.[48]

Through a variety of arrangements, many public libraries receive part-

46. *Houston Chronicle,* 5 May 1979, sec. 6, p. 1.
47. Telephone interview with Jay B. Clark, chief of technical services, Houston (Texas) Public Library, 4 April 1983.
48. "Security in Libraries: Boston Public Hires Guards to Stem Wave of Violence," *Library Journal* 107:584 (15 March 1982).

time police protection, or assistance on demand. One method is to provide a library alarm signal or a telephone that has a direct hookup to the police station switchboard. When the library sends a call for help, the message is relayed to a cruising police car in the neighborhood.

Some libraries have police protection at certain times of the day or in areas where the risks of crime are high. In a number of urban libraries the personnel at the close of the day receive a police cruiser or motorcycle escort as protection as they leave the library for the parking lot.

Police assistance is available to some city librarians to help with the persistent problem of collecting nonreturned materials. One library was instrumental in initiating (through the city attorney) an ordinance that declared it a misdemeanor to retain a library book more than 30 days after receiving a notification that it was overdue. Notices, prepared by the library, are sent to the police department, and an officer delivers them and collects the delinquent books and/or fines. The results have been favorable in terms of book return; the creation of irate patrons, however, places a strain on public relations. One needs to decide if the damage to the image of the library outweighs the costs of the materials rescued.

Other city police forces have formed "book detective squads" to trace patrons when discrepancies occur in their borrowers' cards or they fail to return long-overdue books. One summer in 1982, after the Los Angeles Police Department received a missing-person alert, police were led to the apartment of a Los Angeles Public Library circulation clerk, where they found about 10,000 books stacked from floor to ceiling. Most of the books were stolen from the central library. The clerk was apprehended by the police, fired by the library, and is facing criminal charges.[49] A New York City lawyer made the headlines when he was arrested by the police, after 15,000 New York Public Library books were found in his downtown apartment.[50]

Patterns for the utilization of contract guards differ from one public library to another. Boston Public Library, as mentioned earlier, lost its city police protection due to budget restrictions. Violence increased and the library was confronted with pickpockets, vagrants, and *more* violence. There were muggings in the parking lot and purse-snatchings in the library. In spite of a meager budget, the library hired a contract guard service, and the library's crime rate decreased.[51]

49. "Major Theft at Los Angeles Public," *Wilson Library Bulletin* 57:16 (Sept. 1982).

50. "Library Security Checklist," *Library Security Newsletter* 1:12 (May–June 1975).

51. "Security in Libraries: Boston Public Hires Guards," p. 584.

Some public libraries use part-time contract guard services for the evening hours and Saturday, when crowds are dense and more precaution is needed. Others hire protection service only for the occasional after-hours programs or for Halloween night.

Another aid to security is a silent alarm system that is installed and maintained by a private security company. Automatic response is assured for each alarm, as well as police notification. This measure offers excellent security coverage; however, the cost prohibits its use by most libraries.

The search for appropriate and effective measures of security protection will continue for school, university, and public libraries. Most library administrators, having been shocked into facing reality, are learning to deal with the wide variety of library crimes prevalent in today's society. Experiments are conducted with both inside and outside security measures, or a mixture of both, to find the most effective deterrents to library crime. The safety, reputation, and the very future of our nation's libraries are at stake. We *must* find a way to preserve America's rich library legacy, not only for ourselves but for future generations.

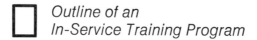

Outline of an In-Service Training Program

Directors and staff members alike must be aware of potential security threats in their libraries. Together, they must seek the best methods for preventing such problems. Also, they must be knowledgeable in dealing with security infractions.

A training program is needed, therefore, to prepare employees to cope effectively with security crises. In-service training needs vary widely in different types and sizes of libraries; however, the following outline might serve as a framework for planning a training program. Obviously, each institution would need to make necessary changes and modifications, appropriate to its unique situation.

I. Establish objectives
    A. Orientation training and security/protection measures for staff members
    B. On-going awareness of security needs
        1. Dealing with disruptive situations
        2. Preventing security breaches

II. Determine "time lines" for in-service sessions
  A. Incorporate into orientation for new employees
  B. Once-a-year review and update for all employees
III. Contents of in-service training program for new employees
  A. Written security policies
    1. Explanation of security policies and procedures (handbooks, manuals, plot plans, floor layouts, etc.)
    2. Identification of security policies of campus, city, county, etc.
  B. Tour of physical facilities (interior and exterior)
    1. Emergency exits
    2. Parking facilities
    3. Lighting system
    4. Fire alarms
    5. Emergency telephones
    6. Ingress and egress
    7. Restroom security
    8. Special collections requiring additional security
    9. Secluded areas
  C. Demonstration of equipment, devices, protection measures
    1. Door locks
    2. Alarm signals
    3. Intercom systems
    4. Fire extinguishers
    5. Electronic security/detection systems
    6. First-aid kits
    7. Automatic signaling devices
    8. Pagers, walkie-talkies
    9. Window locks
    10. Money handling
    11. Central control consoles
    12. Closed-circuit TV
  D. Major security problems and procedures for handling
    1. Theft
    2. Mutilation of materials
    3. Nonreturn of materials
    4. Arson
    5. Disruptive patrons
    6. Medical emergencies
    7. Power outages

       8. Bomb threats

       9. Fires, floods, storms

   E. Staff's responsibilities

       1. To each other

       2. To the patron

       3. To the collection

   F. Auxiliary personnel

       1. Security guards

       2. City or campus police

       3. Fire department

       4. Paramedics

       5. Mental health and social workers

       6. Legal advisors

IV. Follow-up security measures

   A. Continuous reporting of security problems to director

   B. Periodic reevaluation of security policies and procedures (with staff participation)

   C. Posting and dissemination of written policies and procedures

   D. On-going study of impact security measures on public relations

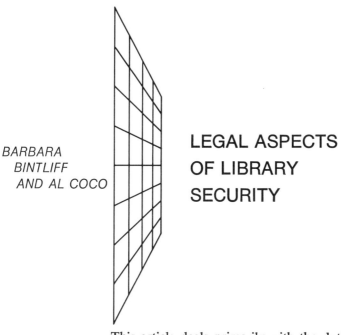

BARBARA
BINTLIFF
AND AL COCO

LEGAL ASPECTS
OF LIBRARY
SECURITY

This article deals primarily with the duties owed by the library to its users to provide a secure and safe atmosphere for both their persons and their belongings. Also discussed are the possible legal consequences involved in carrying out specific security measures and procedures by describing the most typical security-related problems in a library. For example, can denial of access to the library be a violation of a patron's constitutional right? Is searching backpacks, briefcases, and/or purses an invasion of a patron's privacy? Is detention of the person whose property is being searched false imprisonment? These legal issues will be considered in the context of educational institutions, private and public. Although the civil and criminal liability of individuals will be touched upon, the major focus is on the civil liability which the institution may incur.

Excluded from the scope of the article are discussions of the merits of various security systems or precautions; that determination must be left to each institution. Our discussion is limited to liability from the use of security systems. Employer-employee relations will not be covered beyond general discussions of duties owed by an institution to those persons on its premises and the responsibility of the institution for its employees' actions. Federal and state statutes which have heavily impacted

The authors wish to acknowledge the research assistance of Lucien Dhooge and Juliette Levin and the research and editorial assistance of Joseph B. Wilson, all law students at the University of Denver College of Law, and the editorial and typing skills of Georgeann McElhaney.

library activities, especially the Freedom of Information and Privacy acts, are not included except as they may tangentially affect other issues. The confidentiality of circulation files and records is treated in the same manner.

Types of Law. There are two primary categories of law: case law, derived from reported appellate cases, and statutory law, enacted by legislative bodies.

1. Case Law. One aspect of the administration of educational institutions is that many, if not most, legal problems are resolved internally by the institution before they reach the legal system. Typically, probation, suspension, or expulsion/termination of an offending student or employee is the resolution of a disciplinary proceeding. The majority of injury-related claims are generally settled out of court by the parties or their insurance companies. Both the institutional authorities and the private parties involved are normally anxious to avoid court proceedings. The time and money involved are factors which dissuade all but the most insistent party from pursuing a cause past the administrative determination. The publicity and possible damage to the reputation of both parties resulting from a public judicial action frequently provide the final element in the desire to avoid litigation.

The problem with case-law analysis is that it is almost impossible to gain access to information or records of administrative actions. Even those cases which make it to trial are often inaccessible, regardless of the public nature of these proceedings, because, with very few exceptions, the states have no provisions for reporting the outcome of trial cases. In many states there is no requirement that the trial judge prepare a written decision. It isn't until a case reaches the appellate court level that an established system of reporting decisions and opinions exists. We found no reported appellate cases which involve liabilities arising from library security. There are cases, dealing with general school and university security problems, from which we have drawn parallels to libraries.

2. Statutory Law. We find the opposite situation when dealing with statutory law, both at the federal and state level. The federal government and the states have their own systems of statutes, no two of which are alike. In some jurisdictions the laws concerning libraries are extensive; in others, virtually nonexistent. The information presented here is a general summary. Where specific statutes are discussed, they will be identified by state. We cannot emphasize strongly enough that, when problems arise, one should consult an attorney in his or her own state for specific legal advice and guidance.

Legal Terminology. Most often, situations involving library security give rise to potential legal liability for civil actions, called "torts." A tort is "a private or civil wrong or injury, other than a breach of contract, for which the court will provide a remedy in the form of damages."[1] A *tort i*s committed against a person or an identifiable class of people, as distinguished from a *crime,* which is an offense committed against the state. A single act may be both a tort and a crime. For example, if a person steals a car, he or she has committed the crime of theft as well as conversion—a tort against the car's owner. A tort is also distinguishable from a *breach of contract.* A contract arises from an agreement between two or more parties, and any breach is a violation of that agreement. A tort is a violation of a duty imposed by law.

The three basic elements in any tort action are: (1) the existence of an obligation or duty owed by one party to another, (2) a breach or violation of that obligation or duty, and (3) damage or injury as a result of the breach. The primary types of torts include intentional, negligent, and constitutional torts.

A common legal issue arises from the relationship of the library to its employees. When a library user is injured or suffers property damage because of the action or inaction of the library employees, the issue of who bears the ultimate responsibility is raised. Is the employee alone responsible, or must the library bear a portion of the liability? General principles of the law of agency and the area of master-servant relationships bear on these issues. There are two basic forms which this relationship may take in the everyday library setting:

1. Master-servant relationship, or employer-employee relationship, exists where one person employs another to do certain work and exercises control over the other as to method, performance, and duration of employment. As a result of this agency relationship, the doctrine of *respondeat superior* comes into effect; that is, in the course and scope of the employment, the master is legally responsible for the servant's torts. This indirect responsibility is called *vicarious liability.* The majority of library employees, from the director to the part-time student assistant, fit into this category.

2. An independent contractor is one who enters into an employment relationship with another for the completion of a specified piece of work, where the employer has control only over the outcome but not over the methods used. An independent contractor may or may not be the employer's agent. Library-related independent contractors may be consultants, some security or maintenance workers, or independent cataloging service personnel, for example.

The following hypothetical helps explain the difference between the

1. Black's Law Dictionary 1335 (5th ed. 1979).

liability arising from an employer-employee relationship and that from an employer–independent contractor relationship. Assume that a janitor, employed by your institution, after changing several burned-out fluorescent light tubes leaves them leaning against a library table. A student trips over the tubes and is severely lacerated. In this instance, both the janitor and institution may be liable, due to the agency relationship. The injured student may sue not only the library's employee (the janitor) but also the library director, the school, college, or university, and any oversight authority, such as the board of trustees. The primary goal of the plaintiff is to receive recompense for injury in the form of damages. Therefore, the plaintiff sues to reach the person or institution with "deep pockets"—assets sufficient to assure the payment of any judgment rendered.

On the other hand, if the negligent janitor was employed by a private cleaning service, unaffiliated with the institution (making him or her an independent contractor or the agent of an independent contractor), the institution will probably not be liable because it does not exercise direct control over the janitor. The cleaning service, however, will bear responsibility for the janitor's conduct.

The employee–independent contractor distinction bears heavily on potential liability for injury. The library or institution will almost always bear responsibility for the actions of its employees. However, the conduct of an independent contractor will rarely lead to liability of the library or institution. Any library which uses the services of a noninstitutional employee should contact its legal counsel to determine the status of that employee. The library may wish to clarify the nature of the relationship, or even limit its liability through a written contractual agreement.

Crises. While the thrust of this article is on the daily security activities of a library, every institution will experience an occasional crisis which may have security implications. Crises may arise from flooding, tornados, arson, bomb threats, or other extraordinary circumstances. The following discussion is offered to alert the reader to the security implications of a crisis situation.

In considering the liability of the institution in these nontypical situations, we must look to two factors. First, was the institution negligent in creating the crisis? For example, what if a wastebasket fire spreads out of control, injuring several patrons and damaging library books and equipment? If the available fire extinguishers were left unfilled because of unauthorized use by students, the library's action contributed substantially to creation of the crisis condition.

Second, even if the institution did not cause or allow the crisis to occur, did its employees act in such a way as to increase the risk of harm to others? Knowing of a bomb threat or approaching tornado, did the librarians fail to evacuate the building or move people to a safe area because it may have meant leaving the library unattended in the middle of the day?

In a crisis situation, institutional employees are judged by the "reasonable person under the circumstances" test. This is essentially a test of comparison; that is, would the average prudent person act in the same manner when confronted with the same situation? If the answer is no, the institution may face liability for its action or failure to act.

A crisis is, by its very nature, an event for which precise responses cannot be prepared. The best that any library can hope for is enough advance warning to allow its employees to react in an orderly manner. The law does not require a "correct" response; it *does* require one that appeared reasonable at the time.

Specific Liabilities

In the following discussion we will describe different types of security devices and measures and a number of everyday occurrences which give rise to security problems. In each instance we will discuss the possible legal liability of the library and its governing institution or board. In most situations there will be no difference in potential liability between a public and a private institution. If there is a possible distinction, it will be described.

The types of security measures which a library decides to implement must be determined on an individual basis. What is necessary for the large, public, community college in a downtown environment may be wholly inappropriate for a small, private, liberal arts college in a "college town" setting. The community college which is concerned about vandalism, nonstudent use, theft, and possible criminal activity may need to have full-time security guards and to have surveillance cameras and security gates installed; the liberal arts college may need nothing more than continual staffing of the circulation desk to monitor existing students for nonprocessed books. Likewise, the needs of an elementary school library will be different from colleges'. The elementary school may need a library aide to assist in direct supervision of the students, but may not need to implement any other security measures.

Typical Library Security Measures

1. Access to the Library. At the entrance to any library, two security issues may be confronted. First, whether access to the facility can be

had; and second, whether some sort of surveillance by guards, library staff, or cameras is in use.

Frequently, private schools restrict admission to their libraries and other facilities, admitting only their own faculty, students, and staff. The right of a private educational institution to deny the general public access to its property is well recognized[2] (although many private schools have generously opened their library doors to the public). The person who insists on entering a private library, when denied permission, may be guilty of trespass.

The situation is not so clear for publicly supported institutions. The tradition of public access to publicly supported libraries is deep rooted in our society. In many states this access is guaranteed by law, and the Colorado statute is typical:

> The general assembly hereby declares that it is the policy of this state, as a part of its provision for public education, to promote the establishment and development of all types of publicly-supported free library service throughout the state to ensure equal access to information without regard to age, physical or mental health, place of residence, or economic status, to aid in the establishment and improvement of library programs, to improve and update the skills of persons employed in libraries through continuing education activities, and to promote and coordinate the sharing of resources among libraries in Colorado and the dissemination of information regarding the availability of library services.[3]

Under statutes of this sort, state citizens are guaranteed access to publicly supported libraries.

In contrast to statutes that provide for access to publicly financed libraries, most states give the state boards of regents or trustees the power to adopt rules and regulations concerning the control, operation, and management of state educational institutions. Wisconsin law states that the Board of Regents of the University of Wisconsin "may adopt rules . . . to protect the lives, health and safety of persons on property under its jurisdiction and to protect such property and to prevent obstruction of the functions of the system."[4]

Using this type of authority, university and college governing boards routinely declare home economics and science labs, weight-training equipment, and other facilities "off limits" to nonstudents at publicly

2. 75 Am. Jur. 2d *Trespass* § 13 (1974).
3. Colo. Rev. Stat. § 24-90-102 (1973).
4. Wis. Stat. Ann. § 36.11(1)(a) (West Supp. 1982).

supported schools. Few boards have attempted to restrict access to their libraries—although in one state, Washington, access to the University of Washington's Law Library has been restricted. Washington's Administrative Code[5] provides that, in the Law Library,

> (1) . . . reading room and seating on open stack floors are open for use to any person having need of legal materials shelved there. The library is closed to nonlaw students and nonlawyers for use as a study hall (i.e., for use not related to that law library's materials).
> (2) The faculty library is for the use of law faculty only. . . .

Many local school boards have taken similar actions and declared their campuses off limits to all but students of each elementary, junior, or senior high school. Such statutes enable schools legally to control access in accordance with the intended purpose of the facility.

Just as educational institutions are often empowered to restrict access to their libraries, so too are public library boards of trustees. Again, the Colorado statute is typical:

> *Powers and duties of board of trustees.* (1) The board of trustees [of a public library] shall: (a) Adopt such bylaws, rules, and regulations for its own guidance and for the government of the library as it deems expedient; (b) Have supervision, care, and custody of all property of the library. . . .[6]

In the absence of such statutes—or in spite of them, as some contend—a restriction on free access to library facilities may be the basis for a lawsuit on one of several U.S. or state constitutional or statutory grounds. For example, it may be seen as a denial of the U.S. constitutional property right to a public education,[7] an abridgment of one's civil rights,[8] or a violation of a theoretical right to read.[9] It may also violate the provisions of a particular state's constitution or statutes, such as the Colorado statute previously mentioned.

---

5. Wash. Admin. Code R. § 478-168-070 (1980).

6. Colo. Rev. Stat. § 24-90-109 (1982 repl. vol.). Using this authority, the Denver Public Library Board of Trustees closed its doors to non-Denver residents during its fiscal year 1981–82. Non-Denver residents were required to pay users' fees or buy a yearly pass to gain access to DPL; see 107 Lib. J. 212 (1982).

7. *Goss v. Lopez,* 419 U.S. 565 (1975).

8. *Brown v. Board of Education,* 106 W. Va. 476, 146 S.E. 389 (1928).

9. Comment, "Surveillance of Individual Reading Habits: Constitutional Limitations on Disclosure of Library Borrower Lists," 30 Am. U.L. Rev. 275 (1980).

If allowed by statute and constitution, access can be restricted in several ways. Persons may be required to show identification cards, to verbally identify themselves, or to "sign in" by means of a logbook. Once the authority to restrict access is granted, almost any reasonable means to accomplish the end is permissible. However, in at least one state, administrative hearings are required before an institution can restrict access to particular individuals.[10]

2. Surveillance in the Library. A second type of library security issue, which may initially arise upon entry to the library but persists throughout a patron's visit, is surveillance. In society today, the need for some type of "presence" is widely recognized; however, the form which this presence takes is subject to great variations.

Some libraries have resorted to sophisticated electronic surveillance systems, with cameras placed in strategic areas and guards viewing the monitors. Some libraries have stationary or patrolling security personnel. Whenever such systems exist, the question of the patron's right to privacy is raised.

There are two types of privacy rights, those founded on the common law of torts and those based upon the U.S. Constitution. A tortious invasion of privacy may encompass such actions as peering into the windows of a home, electronic eavesdropping, and illegal searches of property in a person's possession.[11] However, it does not include photographing or filming a person in a public place, unless the person retains a strong expectation of privacy despite being in a public area.[12] For example, people entering a courthouse were not allowed to maintain a lawsuit based on intrusion into their privacy by surveillance at the courthouse door; but a woman whose dress was unexpectedly blown upward in a "funhouse" was able to maintain a suit against a photographer for invasion of privacy when he photographed the incident.[13] The test is whether a reasonable person would object to or take offense to the complained-of activity.

Constitutional rights to privacy are of a different nature.[14] They include the Fourth Amendment prohibition against unreasonable searches and seizures, the First Amendment protection of the right to speech and assembly, and the right to engage in a number of highly personal activities

---

10. *Dunkel v. Elkins,* 325 F. Supp. 1235 (D.C. Md. 1971).

11. Prosser, *Handbook on the Law of Torts,* at 802–818 (1971).

12. *Forster v. Manchester,* 410 Pa. 192, 189 A.2d 147 (1963).

13. *Daily Times Democrat v. Graham,* 276 Ala. 380, 162 So. 2d 474 (1964).

14. J. Nowak, R. Rotunda, and J. Young, *Handbook on Constitutional Law,* at 623–635 (1978).

in the areas of marriage,[15] contraception,[16] abortion,[17] reproduction,[18] and the right to possess obscene material in one's own home.[19] These areas may not be exclusive because the U.S. constitutional right to privacy is not definable and is subject to further interpretation or expansion.

While a library user generally enjoys a right to privacy regarding the library materials he or she uses,[20] nothing guarantees him or her a right to be free from a general security screening, so long as the inspection is not without notice.[21] Security measures that are not aimed at one person or a specific group of persons, and are reasonably designed to interfere as little as possible with a patron's expectations of privacy, should be allowable since they further a legitimate interest: preventing theft. For example, one recent case stated that a person who carries contraband (in this case, unpaid-for merchandise) through a department store theft-detection system was not subjected to an unlawful invasion of privacy.[22] Items that are not lawfully within the possession of the individual are not legally protected from reasonable searches (see "Exiting the Library," *infra*).

3. Patron's Use of Library. Once lawful access to the library is gained, most patrons are able to proceed about their business with little or no problem. However, all libraries occasionally encounter the problem patron or employee who creates dangerous situations or threatens injury to others. The security aspects of these situations fall into several categories: the library's responsibility for the safety of the patron's person and his or her property; potential liability of the library or its governing institution for harm done to patrons; and defenses to such potential liability.

A patron may be harmed by either a criminal or a tortious act of another patron or of the library staff. Whether the library must bear responsibility for these acts depends upon who committed them and the manner in which they were committed.

a. Criminal Acts. "An employer is not generally liable for the criminal acts of his employee even though the latter does them in furtherance of his employer's business."[23] For example, a library desk attendant who

---

15. *Loving v. Virginia,* 388 U.S. 1 (1967).

16. *Griswold v. Connecticut,* 381 U.S. 479 (1965); *Eisenstadt v. Baird,* 405 U.S. 438 (1972).

17. *Roe v. Wade,* 410 U.S. 113 (1973).

18. *Skinner v. Oklahoma,* 316 U.S. 535 (1942).

19. *Stanley v. Georgia,* 394 U.S. 557 (1969).

20. Wis. Stat. Ann. § 43.30 (West Supp. 1982).

21. See *Chenkin v. Bellevue Hosp. Ctr.,* 479 F. Supp. 207 (S.D.N.Y. 1979).

22. *Lucas v. United States,* 411 A.2d 360, *reh'g denied,* 414 A.2d 830 (D.C. App. 1980).

23. W. Lafave and A. Scott Jr., *Handbook on Criminal Law,* § 25 at 182 (1972).

unlawfully detains a patron exiting the library will not create criminal liability for the library or school administration, absent a showing of their direction or complicity in the specific act. However, "the same act may be both a crime against the state and a tort against an individual. In such a case . . . there may be both a civil tort action and a criminal prosecution for the same offense."[24] Thus the library may avoid criminal liability while still being liable for a tortious act of its employee. Tort actions are discussed at length below.

Frequently, a library employee needs to prevent a patron from leaving the library when a security alarm sounds or when that patron is suspected of removing library materials improperly. The possibility that some type of criminal or civil liability may be imposed on a library or its employees for this action has not escaped the notice of some state legislatures. At least seven states have passed statutes that remove liability incurred by a library employee who acts in a reasonable manner in detaining a person suspected of concealing or removing library materials.[25] The typical statute is modeled after shoplifting statutes, in which a merchant may detain a suspected thief for questioning or the arrival of police (see "False Arrest/False Imprisonment," *infra*). Laws of this type are excellent protection for librarians and library staff who must deal with the ever-increasing problem of theft of library materials.

Just as a library is not criminally liable for the crimes of its employees, it is also not liable for criminal acts of users or patrons under the same principles. "It is a general principle of criminal law that one is not criminally liable for how someone else acts, unless of course he directs or encourages or aids the other so to act."[26] The library, therefore, cannot be held criminally responsible for injuries or damage to the person or property of its patrons when the injury or damage is caused by others.

There is, however, the possibility that the library could be charged with negligence for lack of supervision or surveillance or for allowing a person, known to be dangerous, to enter the building. This falls into the category of tort liability.

b. Tortious Acts. There are two major areas of tort law: intentional acts and negligent acts. Normally, any case involving torts will be heard in the state courts. There is, however, a fairly new third area, called

---

24. Prosser, *supra* note 11, § 2, at 7.
25. Cal. Penal Code § 490.5 (West Supp. 1981), Iowa Code Ann. § 808.12 (West Supp. 1981), Miss. Code Ann. § 39-3-313 (1981), Ohio Rev. Code Ann. § 2935.041 (page 1982), S.C. Code Ann. § 16-13-332 (Law Co-op. Supp. 1981), Va. Code § 42.1-73.1 (Supp. 1981), Wis. Stat. Ann. § 943.61 (West 1982).
26. W. Lafave and A. Scott Jr., *supra* note 23, at 182.

constitutional torts, which is bringing the federal government into the previously exclusive state arena.

(1) Intentional Torts. An intentional tort is one in which an act that caused injury or damage was done voluntarily, "with intent." This is not to say that the actor *meant* to injure another person. Rather, the intent required encompasses either the intent to effect the desired consequences or the substantial certainty that the act will bring about certain results.[27] The most common intentional torts include defamation and false arrest or imprisonment.

(*a*) Defamation. Defamation is an invasion of a person's reputation and good name by the communication to another of untrue or defamatory statements. Defamation may be oral (slander) or written (libel). The librarian who yells "Stop that thief!" when the library's security gate alarm sounds and the gate locks to stop a patron's exit intends to halt a suspected thief. Others in the vicinity may hear the librarian and, as a result, regard the person in question as a thief, based upon their interpretation of the librarian's actions, tone of voice, and demeanor. If the person is not in actuality a thief, or the library cannot prove such, this action may give rise to charges of defamation (slander).

Charges of defamation have regularly arisen in connection with attempts by shopkeepers to combat shoplifting. Although liability for defamation is common, there are recognized defenses. Obviously, like shopkeepers, librarians should avoid words or acts which indicate accusations of thievery or may be so construed. Additionally, since "publication"—or communication of the defamatory statement to another—is an essential aspect of defamation, particular care should be taken when third parties are present. In a word, discretion is the best defense against defamation. Discretion will tend to both limit the potential for legal action as well as allow those actions taken to be more easily justified if, and when, the library is forced to justify its acts.[28]

(*b*) Assault and Battery. If, in our above example, the angry librarian rushed forward and grabbed or tried to grab the exiting patron and his or her backpack, the librarian may have committed either a battery or an assault. *Battery* is the "unlawful touching of another person without justification or excuse."[29] *Assault* is a reasonable apprehension of the unlawful touching.

Courts have given teachers and administrators considerable leeway in

27. Prosser, *supra* note 11, at 31.
28. Annot., "Defamation: Actionability of Accusation or Imputation of Shoplifting," 29 A.L.R. 3d 961 (1970).
29. Black's Law Dictionary 105 (5th ed. 1979).

disciplining students and have allowed teachers and administrators physically to control students without liability for assault or battery.[30] It is reasonable to assume that librarians fit within the category of teachers or administrators and, so long as the contact is not unnecessarily forceful, librarians at educational institutions may also benefit from this protection. Public librarians, being noneducational government employees, would presumably not be given the same amount of discretion.

Absent a statute relieving librarians and their libraries from responsibility for injuries caused in the reasonable apprehension of suspected miscreants, public libraries, faced with an assault or battery charge, would probably have to rely upon general tort law defenses.

(c) False Arrest/False Imprisonment. Suppose our librarian grabs the exiting patron and takes him or her aside for questioning about the possible unauthorized removal of library materials. If the patron is, or believes he or she is, being restrained from leaving, the patron may have grounds to bring charges of false arrest or false imprisonment. *False arrest or imprisonment* is an unlawful deprivation of a person's liberty or freedom of movement; the two actions are essentially the same.

As previously mentioned, several states have enacted laws specifically limiting the liability of library staffers who reasonably detain persons suspected of theft or destruction of library materials. These statutes are usually modeled after, or included with, the state's shoplifting statutes. Claims of false arrest or imprisonment were commonly pressed against merchants before the passage of the shoplifting statutes,[31] and these statutes have afforded a needed protection. With the advent of security systems and the screening of exiting patrons, it is not unlikely that this type of intentional tort action will find its way into the library setting. In the absence of a statute limiting liability, librarians will have to depend upon general principles of the common law, as developed by the courts, to defend themselves.

(2) Negligent Torts. A second major category of tortious conduct is negligence. *Negligence* is acting, or failing to act, as an ordinary and prudent person would under the circumstances. The types of conditions which may give rise to liability for negligence in library security are centered on the library's duties to supervise its users and employees and its duty to maintain the premises. The courts speak of these duties as the "standard of care" owed to patrons and others. When conduct falls below the required standard of care and injury results, a tort action for negligence may exist.

30. *Simms v. School District No. 1*, 13 Or. App. 119, 508 P.2d 236 (1973).
31. Annot., *supra* note 28.

The standard of care owed by schools (and libraries as subdivisions of the schools) and their employees to persons who come onto the premises is an area of the law which varies from state to state and is in a process of rapid change. The standard of care is generally "ordinary care," similar to that owed by a private landowner to persons who enter his or her property. Libraries and their governing bodies may be liable to patrons and employees for personal or property injury resulting from dangerous conditions or activities on the premises. For example, liability for "slip and fall" cases is fairly common. In one case, when a student slipped on an icy campus sidewalk, the university was held liable for failing in its duty to maintain the premises in an ordinary manner.[32] In another case, a female student fainted in a school lavatory as a result of fumes arising from cleaning agents, which were not properly removed. The court held that the school was liable for burns received when the student's face came into contact with the floor.[33] In each instance, the school authorities failed to conform to the standard of care owed to the students by negligently maintaining the premises.

In general, public libraries and librarians will be subject to the same standards and liabilities as librarians in educational institutions. While the laws will differ among the states, there is rarely, if ever, immunity for the negligent acts of government employees, including public librarians.

Ordinarily, library and school authorities are not liable for personal injuries suffered by students at the hands of others, even if the injury occurs during school hours. For example, Florida Atlantic University, a state-operated university, was not held liable for the abduction and murder of a female student.[34] The court concluded that the university "is not an insurer of the safety of [its students] and is not required to take precautions against a sudden attack from a third person which [it] has no reason to anticipate."[35] Similarly, officials were held not liable for injuries suffered by a student in a Hawaii high school. Although the injured student had been the subject of previous abuse by fellow students, the court dismissed the case, finding that the subsequent assault had been unforeseeable and, thus, the school had not breached the standard of care it owed to him.[36] The courts have justified this on the grounds that there is no *respondeat superior* relationship between the school authorities and the injuring student.

---

32. *Shannon v. Washington University*, 575 S.W.2d 235 (Mo. Ct. App. 1978).
33. *Berrey v. White Wing Services, Inc.*, 44 Colo. App. 506, 619 P.2d 82 (1980).
34. *Relyea v. State*, 385 So. 2d 1378 (Fla. Dist. Ct. App. 1980).
35. *Id.* at 1383.
36. *Kim v. State*, 62 Hawaii 483, 616 P.2d 1376 (1980).

Liability may exist, however, where library or school authorities were negligent in allowing the injuring activity to take place or in failing properly to supervise the activity. The main issue in determining a library's liability for personal injury to a student, resulting from the actions of another student, is whether the library staff could have foreseen the possibility of injury in that particular situation. If the event was foreseeable, the library will, in all likelihood, bear some responsibility for the injury if there was a failure to supervise or prevent the action.

While the states differ on what may or may not be foreseeable, it is generally agreed that a sense of danger, arising from the activity, is sufficient; the specific events leading to injury need not be foreseeable. For example, in the case of *Tarasoff v. Regents*, the University of California was held liable for the wrongful death of one of its students.[37] The court found a duty on the part of university officials to warn the student, Tatiana Tarasoff, that she was in danger when university therapists were told by a patient at the university's Cowell Memorial Hospital of his intention to murder her. No warning was given to her, and the breach of this duty gave rise to liability when she was subsequently murdered by the patient.

The *Tarasoff* case is an example of an institution failing to act. Liability can also arise from incomplete or unreasonable action. In *Jesik v. Maricopa County Comm. College Dist.*, the community college was held liable for the wrongful death of a student who had reported death threats against him.[38] Jesik, who had had an argument with another student during registration in the college's gym, reported the ensuing death threat to the appropriate security official. The student who made the threats left the building and returned to the gymnasium with a briefcase containing a gun. Although he was stopped, he was not searched by security officials, even though he was known to have threatened Jesik. This failure to exercise due care and act on the known threat resulted in direct liability for the college when Jesik was shot and killed.

Even if the library is not directly responsible for injury to a student or patron (caused by another), the library may be liable for the failure to supervise its patrons adequately. Two determinations must be made here: whether the library has a duty to supervise in the situation, and whether such duty was satisfied.

The library and its employees are not guarantors of the safety of patrons and staff, and generally, the duty owed to them is that of ordinary care. Their actions should be comparable to those of a reasonable

---

37. 17 Cal. 3d 425, 551 P.2d 334, 131 Cal. Rptr. 14 (1976).
38. 125 Ariz. 543, 611 P.2d 125 (1980).

and prudent person under similar circumstances. The reasonableness of the actions will depend on the time, place, and nature of the activity. When young children are involved, the library must exercise greater care than when high school or college students or adult users are involved.

Courts are reluctant to impose liability if supervision could not have prevented the injury; but if large numbers of people regularly gather in one area, failure to supervise may result in liability. For example, when a young student was injured on a "jungle gym," it was found that additional supervision may have prevented the accident. In particular, closer supervision may have detected that the student was wearing mittens, contrary to safety regulations.[39] However, failure to supervise in strict accordance with school district "handbooks" has been held not to constitute negligence in itself.[40]

The requirement that libraries "supervise" has direct security implications. A visible authority figure can reduce vandalism and other activities which may threaten the safety of the library's users. The supervisor may identify or discover maintenance problems, such as wet floors or broken windows, which can injure patrons, or permit unauthorized entry or exit. The supervisor must avoid infringing on the privacy of the library's patrons, although this is not too difficult because the library user's expectation of privacy is considerably less in the library than at home.

(3) Constitutional Torts. The constitutional tort is rapidly expanding in scope and importance. A constitutional tort suit involves an activity of the library or institution or an employee which violates the rights, privileges, and immunities guaranteed individuals by the Fourteenth Amendment of the U.S. Constitution or the Federal Civil Rights Act of 1965.[41] These are also referred to as "civil rights torts." Cases in this area frequently involve claims of racial or sexual discrimination, although there are other areas of law involved.[42]

In order to bring a constitutional or civil rights tort case, the injured party must show that there was "state action"—a relationship between the state or federal government and the library. This is easy to establish for a public institution which is funded and controlled by the state and staffed by state employees. State action is not as easily identified at a private institution since there must be a finding of significant state involvement with the conduct in question. State action has been found

39. *Hommel v. Carey,* 66 A.D.2d 967, 412 N.Y.S.2d 57 (1978).
40. *Joseph v. Monroe,* 419 A.2d 927 (Del. 1980).
41. 42 U.S.C. § 1983 (1976).
42. Annot., "Action of Private Institutions of Higher Education as Constituting State Action, or Action under Color of Law, for Purposes of the Fourteenth Amendment and 42 U.S.C.S. § 1983," 37 A.L.R. Fed. 601 (1978).

through various analyses, including the fact that most private schools and colleges are incorporated, and corporations are allowed and regulated by the state; the fact that the government provides financial aid to students of the institution; the fact that the state has certain minimum requirements for accreditation which are met by that institution; the fact that the institution fulfills a "public function" by educating state citizens and providing services and facilities for public use; the fact that a library is a depository for U.S. or state government documents; and the fact that the state has the authority to regulate the complained-of activity. Courts have been more willing to find state action where particularly offensive conduct, such as racial discrimination, is involved.[43]

Physical injury is rarely a component of a constitutional or civil rights tort; the tort damage is more often of an intangible nature, including infringement of the right to liberty, which includes the right to a good name and reputation,[44] the right to a public education,[45] a theoretical right to read,[46] the right to be secure against unreasonable searches and seizures under the Fourth Amendment, and the right to be treated equally and with due process of law.[47]

The two most common security-related activities that give rise to charges of a constitutional or civil rights tort involve ejecting a student from the library and searching exiting patrons. (Searches will be covered in the section "Exiting the Library.") When a publicly supported library finds it necessary to request that an unauthorized or disruptive patron leave the premises, the request is frequently allowed by statute or administrative regulation, similar to that enacted by the state of Maryland:

> (a) . . . The president, principal, or governing board of any public institution of elementary, secondary, or higher education may deny access to the buildings or grounds of the institution to any person . . . who acts in a manner that disrupts or disturbs the normal educational functions of the institution.
>
> (c) . . . A person is guilty of a misdemeanor and on conviction is subject to a fine not exceeding $1000, imprisonment not exceeding 6 months, or both if he: . . .

43. There is also a question of whether the state and its agencies can be sued on a federal constitutional question. The Eleventh Amendment has traditionally been a bar to suits under § 1983, but more recently the courts have allowed suits based on the Fourteenth Amendment. See "Developments in the Law—Section 1983 and Federalism," 90 Harv. L. Rev. 1133 (1977).

44. *Board of Regents v. Roth,* 408 U.S. 564 (1972).

45. *Goss v. Lopez, supra* note 7.

46. Comment, *supra* note 9.

47. *Dunkel v. Elkins, supra* note 10.

(2) Fails or refuses to leave the grounds of any of these institutions after being requested to do so by an authorized employee of the institution. . . .[48]

Many states have similar statutes, and those who break them may be guilty of trespass. Generally, this type of statute will be held constitutional, as long as it is clearly written and provides notice of what may be prohibited behavior.[49]

Many states also have statutes that outline the powers of public library boards of trustees to control access. For example, Washingon state provides that "[e]very [public] library . . . shall be free for the use of the inhabitants of the governmental unit in which it is located, subject to such reasonable rules and regulations as the trustees find necessary to assure the greatest benefit to the greatest number,"[50] and "[the] board of trustees of a [public] library, under such rules and regulations as it may deem necessary and upon such terms and conditions as may be agreed upon, may allow nonresidents of the governmental unit in which the library is situated to use the books thereof."[51]

Other states have broader statutes, covering all public buildings, which provide public employees with the authority to restrict access. For example, Maryland provides that

[a]ny person refusing or failing to leave a public building or grounds . . . upon being requested to do so by an authorized employee . . . if the surrounding circumstances are such as to indicate to a reasonable man that such person has no apparent lawful business to pursue at such place or is acting in a manner disruptive of and disturbing to the conduct of normal business by such agency or institution, shall be guilty of a misdemeanor.[52]

As long as the employee acts reasonably in requesting a person to leave, there should be no grounds to bring a suit based on a tortious denial of access where public libraries can invoke the authority of either of these types of statutes.

Where no authorizing statute or regulation exists or where no reasonably necessary purpose exists for requesting a library user to leave, the library may be open to a tort charge of discrimination. This is the same

48. Md. Educ. Code Ann. § 26-102 (1978).
49. *Kirstel v. State,* 13 Md. App. 482, 284 A.2d 12 (1971), *appeal dismissed,* 409 U.S. 943 (1972).
50. Rev. Code of Wash. Ann. § 27.12.270 (1982).
51. Rev. Code of Wash. Ann. § 27.12.280 (1982).
52. Md. Code Ann. art. 27 § 577A(2) (1974).

type of action which would be brought in a denial of access case, as described above. Nevertheless, courts have been willing to allow school authorities the power to eject unauthorized or disruptive persons from school grounds. For example, a University of Kentucky student, protesting the presence of U.S. Defense Intelligence Agency recruiters on campus, refused to leave a building after being so requested. His conviction of trespassing was affirmed on appeal, the court stating:

> The privilege of an enrolled student to use and occupy the property of a school is and should be subject to the will of its governing authorities. If he is told to stay out of a particular room, building, or familiar trysting place, he enters it as a trespasser. Likewise, if he is directed to leave it he remains as a trespasser.[53]

4. Exiting the Library. Whether the patron has been requested to leave the library or leaves at the natural conclusion of his or her business, several security-related issues arise when this patron approaches the exit. Once again, we confront the issue of surveillance by guards or cameras and the related privacy issues. Also, we encounter the question of whether the patron's briefcase or backpack can be legally searched and/or the patron detained if suspected of unauthorized activities. The possibility of an intentional tort is present, as is the possibility of a constitutional or civil rights tort.

The issues surrounding surveillance have been discussed previously. As long as the surveillance is not unnecessarily intrusive and notices concerning the use of surveillance methods have been posted, it will generally be allowed by the courts. However, once the surveyor decides it is necessary to act upon information discovered through the surveillance, a new area of potential liability comes into play.

Suppose that, upon visual observation, a library employee is reasonably convinced that an exiting patron is attempting to remove library materials in an unauthorized manner. The employee, undoubtedly acting within the scope of his or her employment, will attempt to stop the patron for questioning or retrieval of the materials. The manner in which this is accomplished may be determinative of the issue of liability.

The employee who roughly seizes and drags the patron to the side may be liable for the intentional tort of battery or false imprisonment. If the employee makes such statements as "Caught you, you sneaky thief!" or "Bring back that book you're trying to steal!" he or she may be liable for the intentional tort of defamation, an invasion of privacy by placing

---

53. *O'Leary v. Commonwealth,* 441 S.W.2d 150, 157 (Ky. Ct. App. 1969).

the patron in a false light in the public eye, or a constitutional tort by injuring the good name or reputation of the patron. In any of these situations, the library employee and the institution may be liable for any damage suffered, including emotional distress or humiliation, and also for punitive damages, because the library employee was empowered to stop patrons at the exit.

Many libraries engage in a systematic procedure of searching the belongings of exiting students and users in an attempt to curtail theft. Other libraries use electronic surveillance, either cameras or security alarm systems, to achieve their purpose. In each instance the library must be aware of the potential for violation of its patrons' and students' U.S. constitutional right to be protected from unreasonable searches and seizures. The Fourth Amendment to the U.S. Constitution guarantees to all citizens the right to be free from unreasonable searches and seizures. The law in this area is voluminous and highly detailed, but there are basic principles which are uniformly applicable.

A *search* can be defined as an intrusion into or observation of a person's activities which infringes upon his or her reasonable expectation of privacy. The search may be of the person's body or possessions; it may involve a physical examination or a visual observation by machine or in person. However, the U.S. Constitution's Fourth Amendment prohibits only unreasonable searches, not any and every inspection. The reasonableness of any search will depend upon its particular circumstances.

Any search involving state action requires a search warrant. A search that has not been authorized by warrant is presumed invalid unless one of a few narrow exceptions is met. Actions by private citizens, acting in their private capacity, are not governed by search and seizure rules. Therefore, such items as noncirculating rare books or plates or pages removed from books, which are discovered or seized as a result of an illegal search by state action, cannot be used as evidence in a trial, although they can be used by both public and private libraries in institutional or administrative disciplinary cases.[54]

The right to engage in a general surveillance program has been recognized, but a general right to detain exiting patrons and physically search them is not so clear. As previously mentioned, at least seven states have enacted laws which shield library employees from civil and/or criminal liability for a reasonable detention of persons suspected of removing library materials without permission. Under these laws, library employees can generally search for library materials without obtaining a warrant.

---

54. Annot., "Admissability, in Criminal Cases, of Evidence Obtained by Search Conducted by School Official or Teacher," 49 A.L.R.3d (1973).

Apparently, library employees in other states act at their own risk when they detain suspected persons.

Many libraries routinely inspect the backpacks, briefcases, and parcels of exiting patrons. This practice brings up the question of the constitutionality of such security measures. The Fourth Amendment of the U.S. Constitution guarantees the right to be free from unreasonable searches and seizures;[55] many state constitutions guarantee the same right.[56] In determining whether a particular search violates a constitutional right and thereby results in tort liability, two factors must be considered: did the exiting patron have a reasonable expectation of privacy in the articles he or she was carrying, and was the search reasonable under the circumstances?

The expectation of privacy with respect to items rightfully in a person's possession is well recognized.[57] Backpacks, shopping bags, purses, and other items people commonly carry are in the sphere of privacy surrounding every person. The question, then, is whether the search in question is reasonable.

Several criteria by which to judge reasonableness were mentioned in a recent case, including the need for adequate advance notice of the inspection policy and the availability of an alternative procedure in which parcels can be checked before one enters the building. If this procedure is used, all searches can be avoided, thereby preserving the right to privacy.[58] Other factors to consider in determining reasonableness are whether a less obtrusive method of inspecting is available; whether the necessity for searching outweighs the expectation of privacy; whether the search carries the implication of guilt or is accomplished on a random, nonaccusatory level; and whether items other than library property are sought or seized. (Libraries that use a manual inspection system should carefully evaluate their procedures to make sure their actions are as minimally intrusive as possible.)

A new legal question is presented by the use of electronic security-gate systems, where an alarm sounds and/or a gate locks if a patron attempts an unauthorized removal of library materials. This situation is similar to the use of electronic detection devices in stores to detect shoplifting.

In a recent case in the District of Columbia Appeals Court, it was decided that the search of a woman was not in violation of her Fourth

55. U.S. Const. amend. IV.

56. See Colo. Const. art. II, sec. 7.

57. *Arkansas v. Sanders,* 442 U.S. 753 (1979); *Lucas v. United States, supra* note 22; *Chenkin v. Bellevue Hosp. Ctr., supra* note 21.

58. *Chenkin v. Bellevue Hosp. Ctr., supra* note 21.

Amendment rights, after she set off the security alarm upon leaving a clothing store. She was carrying merchandise with the store's inventory-control tag still attached, indicating that the merchandise had not been properly purchased. The court stated that the intrusion caused by the electronic search was not unreasonable when weighed against the economic damage caused by shoplifting and the inability to control shoplifting by other means.[59] The court stated that although a right to privacy extends to parcels and packages in a person's possession, it does not extend to articles which they have no right to possess. The court pointed out that an electronic system, such as that used by the store, did not "search or scan generally for items in which the subject has a proprietary interest. It reveals nothing about the subject or his belongings other than whether he is carrying store merchandise with live tags. . . ."[60] Thus the search was held to be only of items not properly possessed by the customer. The *Lucas* case allowed a search by machine, even though "state action" was found through the presence of security guards empowered to arrest.

It is reasonable to expect that a similar result will be reached in like cases in other states, and should extend to the type of security systems used in libraries.

5. Library Defenses. As in any other type of lawsuit, the defenses of the library employee and the library to charges of wrongdoing will vary with the circumstances of each case. There is, however, an established body of law which may limit the scope or even preclude a lawsuit against most educational and governmental institutions. For public entities, the governing principle is *sovereign immunity*; private, nonprofit institutions may be able to use the doctrine of *charitable immunity*.

The doctrine of sovereign immunity has its roots in ancient times, when the king was immune from any suit brought by his subjects. It has evolved into a bar to lawsuits against the government by private citizens, absent a statute allowing such suits. The federal government and all the states now allow citizens to sue in tort for damages for personal injuries under certain conditions, but most jurisdictions have retained some form of sovereign immunity, which usually includes public schools, colleges, and universities. Other governmental entities that generally are covered by sovereign immunity include public hospitals, state fairs, and prisons. Presumably, public libraries would be afforded the same protection. Any immunity from suit cannot be waived, but may be inapplicable if the

---

59. *Lucas v. United States, supra* note 22.
60. *Id.* at 364.

governmental employee who caused the injury acted willfully or purposely.[61]

The scope of the protection offered by sovereign immunity varies dramatically from state to state; and within each state, differences in immunity are often found between the state government and cities, counties, and municipal corporations. Some states have abolished sovereign immunity in favor of allowing citizens to recover damages for injuries up to the amount of liability insurance carried by the state or other governmental entity.

Even in jurisdictions in which sovereign immunity has been abolished or severely limited, the courts have been reluctant to impose liability for injuries caused by the exercise of judgment by school authorities. For example, a school district in Illinois was not liable for the allegedly negligent actions of the high school basketball coach when he allowed an overly aggressive player to remain on the floor and, subsequently, injure another player. The court said the judgment of the coach should be subject to neither the second-guessing of the legal system nor the fear of incurring liability on his employer.[62] Similarly, maintenance, repair, and construction of school buildings, equipment, and grounds are considered governmental functions, and schools have frequently been declared immune from suits for injury caused by unsafe conditions on the premises unless the condition is legally declared a nuisance.

The law of charitable immunity from tort liability for private schools, colleges, and universities is in a confused state.[63] A growing number of state courts have eliminated immunity for these private institutions, declaring that they must bear the same liability as any other private entity. States which recognize *some* form of the doctrine have delimited its scope, from its previously unlimited character.

Where charitable immunity is recognized, the school must prove that it is, indeed, a charitable institution. This is generally shown where the purpose of the school is to serve nonprofit public purposes rather than private gain. The fact that the school charges tuition, carries liability insurance, or conducts income-producing activities does not mean that it is noncharitable, but if profitmaking is an objective of the institution, it will be denied charitable immunity.

Jurisdictions differ on the scope of charitable immunity. For example,

---

61. Annot., "Modern Status of Doctrine of Sovereign Immunity as Applied to Public Schools and Institutions of Higher Learning," 33 A.L.R. 3d 703 (1970).

62. *Fustin v. Board of Education,* 101 Ill. App. 2d 113, 242 N.E. 2d 308 (1968).

63. Annot., "Immunity of Private Schools and Institutions of Higher Learning from Liability in Tort," 38 A.L.R. 3d 480 (1971).

some states allow a school's employees and visitors to sue for injury but prohibit such suits by students, who are considered beneficiaries of the school's charitable purposes. Other states have allowed recovery only for certain types of injury, for example, injury caused by willful acts of employees or through use of nontrust or endowment property. In some states the doctrine has been eliminated and the liability of an institution is determined in the same manner as for a private party.

If the institution cannot claim sovereign or charitable immunity as a bar to a lawsuit, it must rely on the same types of defense any private party could use. These might include authorization of the complained-of acts by statute or administrative regulation, knowledge or consent of the complaining party, the necessity of taking immediate action, or the absence of any duty to the injured party. The library might also deny responsibility for the acts of its employee, claiming the employee was acting outside the scope of his or her employment.

The absence of case law in the area of library security makes it necessary to resort to general legal principles to predict the probable outcome of any legal action. In general, we can assume that a library and its governing institution will usually not be liable for criminal acts or intentional torts of its students or employees or the behavior of independent contractors in is employment. However, each situation must be judged separately.

The areas in which the library has the greatest potential liability are negligent and constitutional torts. The outcome of these cases depends almost entirely on the facts; there are no clear-cut rules governing tort liability. To identify the applicable law, the courts and attorneys of each state must identify and analyze the cases already decided to find general trends in similar situations. Because the basic standard used to determine tort liability compares the actions actually taken to the conduct of the average, prudent person, there is rarely a "right" or "wrong" response. As long as the actions were reasonable in the circumstances, individual and institutional liability will probably be minimal. The best advice is to use common sense when confronted with a problem.

Schools and institutions should have some sort of training to alert their employees to potential security-related issues, possibly as part of their employee orientation program. Institutional liability insurance coverage should be evaluated. Above all, become acquainted with the legal counsel provided for the library or institution. Contact your lawyer to discuss any questions relating to your library's security. If an accident or incident occurs, contact your lawyer as soon as possible to ascertain your legal rights and minimize your liability.

☐ Questions to Ask an Attorney

One of the first things any library administrator should do is determine the nature and extent of the legal counsel provided by the library's governing institution. Many colleges and universities have a full-time attorney, with offices on campus; others keep an attorney on retainer and consult with him or her whenever the need arises. Private schools usually have similar arrangements. Public schools and public libraries generally have access to the services of the city or county attorney.

Once the attorney has been identified, he or she should be requested to review the operations and policies of the library. In the process, the library administrator may wish to ask the following questions:

1. If there are nonpermanent employees working in or for the library, does their employment contract specify their status in relation to the library (i.e., is the employee an independent contractor or a regular employee)?

2. What is the status of the state's sovereign immunity or charitable immunity doctrine in regard to libraries? Can either of these doctrines be relied upon to bar a lawsuit against the library or its employees?

3. Does the state have a library security statute which will protect a library employee from civil and/or criminal liability if the employee believes he or she is acting to prevent a theft? Can policies be developed to help guide the employees' response to this type of situation?

4. Does the state require insurance coverage of libraries? How does this affect the library's potential liability for injuries to patrons?

5. Can the library restrict its use under state law or local regulation? What steps must be followed to implement or enforce use policies?

6. Are the surveillance or search techniques currently being used legal? Are they necessary? Can another, less obtrusive policy be implemented?

7. Are signs warning of electronic surveillance, exit searches, etc., necessary? What constitutes a legally sufficient sign?

☐ Questions to Ask an Insurance Agent

Although most libraries are covered by insurance to some extent, they are usually included in collective policies issued to the educational institution or governmental body as a whole. It may have been a number of

years since an insurance agent visited the library. The library administrator may wish to arrange an on-site inspection tour with the insurance
company's representative to discuss the coverage and limitations of the
current insurance arrangements. During the tour the following questions
could be posed:

1. Is the insurance required by the state adequate to cover potential
liability?

2. If the library has been remodeled or rearranged, has the insurance
company been notified? Has the policy been changed to reflect the modifications?

3. Can the insurance agent make any suggestions about ways to arrange furniture and workspaces to alleviate otherwise isolated seating or
workspaces which may be conducive to assault, accidents, etc.?

4. Can the insurance agent provide on-the-job training programs to
alert employees to potential security problems?

5. Can conditions (locked emergency exits, missing warning signs)
which could affect potential liability be identified and corrected?

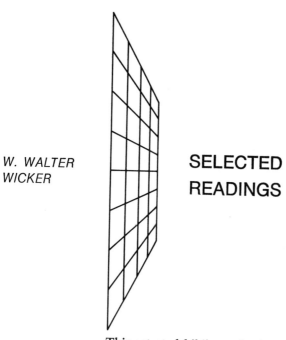

W. WALTER
WICKER

SELECTED READINGS

This selected bibliography is arranged in the following categories: Archives and Special Collections, Computers, Detection Systems, Disasters, Fire, Insurance, Law, Security, and Theft and Mutilation. The Law section was prepared by Barbara Bintliff and Al Coco.

Archives and Special Collections

Adams, Randolph G. "The Character and Extent of Fugitive Archival Materials," *American Archivist* 2:85–96 (April 1939).

Albert, S. C. " 'Multum in Parvo': Application of Microfilm in Cathedral Libraries," *Microfilm Review* 10:153–158 (Summer 1981).

American Library Association. Association of College and Research Libraries. "Guidelines for the Security of Rare Books, Manuscripts, and Other Special Collections," *College and Research Libraries News* #3:90–91 (March 1982).

Coulson, Anthony J. "Conservation of Photographs: Some Thoughts and References," *Art Libraries Journal* 5:5–11 (Spring 1980).

Everitt, Cynthia A. "Security in Map Collections," *Library Trends* 29:493–498 (Winter 1981).

Fennelly, L. J. *Museum, Archive, and Library Security*. Boston: Butterworth, 1983. 891p.

Gandert, S. "Library and Archival Crime: Some Recent Larcenies, Misappropriations and Other Peccadilloes," *Library and Archival Security* 4:31–34 (Winter 1982).

Harrison, Helen P. "Preservation of Moving Pictures and Sound Carriers," *Art Libraries Journal* 5:13–20 (Spring 1980).

Land, Robert H. "Defense of Archives against Human Foes," *American Archivist* 19:121–138 (April 1956).

Mason, Philip P. "Archival Security: New Solutions to an Old Problem," *American Archivist* 38:477–492 (Oct. 1975).

Price, Cheryl A. "Document Examination in American Archives," *Special Libraries* 68:299–304 (Sept. 1977).

Pruett, Nancy J. "Handling Map Collections in a Geological Library: Advice from Map Experts," *Western Association of Map Libraries Information Bulletin* 12:144–151 (March 1981).

Randall, G. E. "The Inventory of a Special Library Collection," *Special Libraries* 63:13–134 (March 1972).

Rendell, K. W. "Proof of Ownership: A Dealer's Perspective," *A B Bookman's Weekly* 67:339–340 (19 Jan. 1980).

Samuel, Evelyn. "Protection of Library and Archival Material: A Case Study—New York University's Institute of Fine Arts," *Library and Archival Security Newsletter* 2:1–6 (Oct. 1979).

Smith, Gaye. "Security in the Art Library," *Art Libraries Journal* 5:26–32 (Spring 1980).

Strickler, Anthony Ross. "Implementation of Process Management for a Secure Archival Storage System," Monterey, Calif.: Naval Postgraduate School, 1981. 228p.

Walch, Timothy. *Archives and Manuscripts: Security.* Chicago: Society of American Archivists, 1977.

Ward, Nicholas D. "Photography: Art Form or Legal Forum?" *Picturescope* 28: 15–16 (Winter 1980).

Computers

"Computer Information Security and Protection, January 1975–May, 1981." Washington, D.C.: National Technical Information Service, 1981. PB81-866402.

Dewey, Patrick R. "Problems in the Personal Computer Center," *Small Computers in Libraries* 2:1–2 (April 1982).

Goldstein, Charles M., and Richard S. Dick. "Automation Support for Collection Management and Control," *Collection Management* 4:1–2, 85–99 (Spring–Summer 1982).

Johnson, Davis G. "Ethical and Legal Aspects of Computer-Based Student Information Systems." Washington, D.C.: ERIC, 1980. ED 190094. 10p.

"Library Document Control System (Designed to Maintain Control of Computer Tapes, Printouts and Other Documents and Detect Unauthorized Removal)," *Microform Review* 10:139–140 (Summer 1981).

Nunes, John L. "The Electronic Librarian," *College Management* 7:26–27 (March 1972).

Pitcher, Hugh H. W. "Data Protection for All," *Information Technology* 78:727–732 (1978).

Detection Systems

Bahr, A. H. *Book Thefts and Library Security Systems, 1981–1982.* White Plains, N.Y.: Knowledge Industry Publications, 1981. 156p.

Beaman, L. A. "Security Systems for School Media Centers," *Indiana Media Journal* 1:20–22 (Fall 1978).

Bommer, Michael, and Bernard Ford. "A Cost-Benefit Analysis for Determining the Value of an Electronic Security System," *College and Research Libraries* 35:270–279 (July 1974).

Davis, DiAnne. "The Economical Feasibility of Installing a Book Detection System at Cottonwood High School." Washington, D.C.: ERIC, 1977. ED144603. 77p.

Hatfield, F. S., and J. P. Klasing. "Electronic Security Systems Do Work," *School Library Journal* 26:51 (Nov. 1979).

Kaske, Neal K. *A Study of Book Detection Systems' Effectiveness and the Level of Missing Materials at the University of California, Berkeley.* Berkeley: University Library, University of California, 1978. 81p.

Knight, N. H. "Library Security Systems Come of Age." *American Libraries* 9:229–232 (April 1978).

————. "Theft Detection Systems—A Survey," *Library Technology Reports* 12:575–690 (Nov. 1976).

————. "Theft Detection Systems for Libraries Revisited," *Library Technology Reports* (May 1979).

Michalko, James, and Toby Heidtmann. "Evaluating the Effectiveness of an Electronic Security System," *College and Research Libraries* 39:263–267 (July 1978).

Molesworth, Bill. "Tattle Tape Security System," *APLA Bulletin* 45:20 (Sept. 1981).

Romeo, Louis J. "Electronic Theft Detection Systems, Part I," *Library and Archival Security* 2:nos. 3–4 (1978).

————. "Electronic Theft Detection Systems, Part II: University Libraries," *Library and Archival Security* 3:1–23 (Spring 1980).

————. "Electronic Theft Detection Systems, Part III: High School Libraries," *Library and Archival Security* 3:1–16 (Summer 1980).

————. "Electronic Theft Detection Systems, Part IV: Public Libraries," *Library and Archival Security* 3:1–22 (Fall–Winter 1980).

————. "Electronic Theft Detection Systems, Part V: Medical and Law Libraries," *Library and Archival Security* 3:99–114 (Fall–Winter 1980).

"Security Systems in Use: Wisconsin Libraries/Media Centers Show Good Results," *Wisconsin Library Bulletin* 76:133–134 (May/June 1980).

Sheridan, Robert N., and Pleasant W. Martin. *Results of Tests Conducted to Determine the Need for a Book Theft Deterrent Device and the Ability*

of the "Tattle Tape" Electronic Book Detection to Reduce Book Theft.
Levittown, N.Y.: Council on Library Resources, 1972.

Shirley, Don. "Library Material Security Systems: A School District's Experience," *School Library Journal* 23:38–41 (April 1977).

Ungarelli, D. L. "Cost-Benefits of a Book Detection System: A Comparative Study," in Quantitative Measurement and Dynamic Library Service, pp. 149–158. Phoenix: Oryx Press, 1978.

Vincent, Ida. "Electronic Security Systems in Libraries: Measuring the Costs and Benefits," *Australian Library Journal* 27:231–236 (1 Sept. 1978).

Disasters

Bohem, Hilda. *Disaster Prevention and Disaster Preparedness.* University of California Systemwide Administration, Office of the Assistant Vice President, 1978. 23p.

Buchanan, Sally. "Disaster Prevention and Action," *Oklahoma Librarian* 30:35–41 (Oct. 1980).

―――. "Disaster: Prevention, Preparedness and Action," *Library Trends* 30:241–52 (Fall 1981).

Carey, Margaret, and Others. *Emergency Manual, Cornell University Library.* Ithaca: Cornell University Library, 1976. 35p.

Michael, Douglas O. *Disaster Preparedness Manual.* Auburn, N.Y.: Cayuga County Community College, Bourke Memorial Library, 1981. 30p.

Pettit, Katherine D. *Emergencies and Problems: A Procedures Manual for Trinity University Library.* San Antonio: Trinity University Library, 1981. 73p.

Porter, Barry L. *Iowa Statewide Disaster Recovery Plan.* Des Moines: Iowa State Library Commission, 1981. 21p.

Spawn, William. "Disasters: Can We Plan for Them? If Not, How Can We Proceed?" In *Preservation of Library Materials*, pp. 24–29. New York: Special Libraries Association, 1980.

Fire

Fortson-James, Judith. "Fire Protection for Libraries," *Catholic Library World* 53:211–213 (Dec. 1981).

Galloway, Sue, and Ruth Heifetz. "Environmental Hazards in the Library," *Technicalities* 1:12–15 (Sept. 1981).

Hoffman, F. W., and L. McDaniel-Hariston. "Fire in the Library: An Informal Case Study with a Checklist for Minimizing Disastrous Consequences," *South-Eastern Librarian* 32:79–84 (Winter 1982).

"Is Your Library Safe from Fire?" *American School and University* 52:60–63 (April 1980).

Jordan, R. "Sifting the Ashes: Fire in the Library," *Tennessee Librarian* 34:15–19 (Summer 1982).

"Library Fire Specialist's Study Pinpoints Patterns in Arson," *Library Journal* 107:496 (1 March 1982).

Morris, John. "Is Your Library Safe from Fire?" *American School and University* 52:60–63 (April 1980).

_____. "Is Your Library Safe from Fire?" *Library and Archival Security* 3:129–145 (Fall–Winter 1980).

_____. *Managing the Library Fire Risk.* 2d ed. Berkeley: University of California, Office of Risk Management and Safety, 1979. 147p.

Wright, Gordon H. "Fire! Anguish! Dumb Luck! or, Contingency Planning," *Canadian Library Journal* 36:254–260 (Oct. 1979).

Insurance

American Library Association. Library Technology Project. *Protecting the Library and Its Resources: A Guide to Physical Protection and Insurance.* Chicago: American Library Association, 1963. 322p.

"Insurance," *Library and Archival Security* 4 #1&2:118–121 (1982).

Kenneweg, R. "Developing a Library Insurance Program," *Library Security Newsletter* 2:11–14 (Summer 1978).

Myers, G. E. *Insurance Manual for Libraries.* Chicago: American Library Association, 1977.

Ungarelli, D. L. "Insurance for Libraries," *American Library Association (ALA) Yearbook* 1978:154–155; 1979:136–137; 1980:165–166; 1981: 155–156.

Law

Bolmeier, Edward C. *The School in the Legal Structure.* 2d ed. Cincinnati: W. H. Anderson, 1973.

_____, ed. *Legal Issues in Education.* Charlottesville: Michie, 1970.

Brand, Marvine. "Security of Academic Library Buildings," *Library and Archival Security* 3:39 (1980).

Brubacher, John Seiler. *The Courts and Higher Education.* San Francisco: Jossey-Bass, 1971.

Burns Security Institute. *National Survey on Library Security.* New York: Burns Security Institute, 1973.

Chambers, M. M. *The Colleges and the Courts, 1962–1966.* Danville, Ill.: Interstate Printers and Publishers, 1967.

Davis, Russell J. "Validity, under Federal Constitution, of Search Conducted as Condition of Entering Public Building," Annot. 53 *A.L.R. Fed.* 888 (1981).

Edwards, Harry T., and Virginia Davis Nordin. *Higher Education and the Law*. Cambridge, Mass.: Institute of Educational Management, 1979.

_____. *Higher Education and the Law*. Cambridge, Mass.: Institute of Educational Management, 1980.

_____. *Higher Education and the Law*. Cambridge, Mass.: Institute of Educational Management, 1981.

Fritze, Roger L. "Know Who Is Liable," *Security Management* 26/5:43 (May 1982). Discussion of "joint employer" status and consequent degress of liability.

Gee, E. Gordon, and David I. Sperry. *Education Law and the Public Schools: A Compendium*. Boston: Allyn and Bacon, 1978.

Genzel, G. H. "Defamation: Actionability of Accusation or Imputation of Shoplifting." Annot. 29 *A.L.R.3d* 961 (1970).

Gibson, Joseph. "Visitor's Refusal to Leave Premises," *Cleveland State Law Review* 21:154 (1972).

Ghent, Jeffrey F. "Validity of Campus Trespass Statute." Annot. 50 *A.L.R.3d* 340 (1973).

Hazard, William R. *Education and the Law*. 2d ed. New York: Free Press, 1978.

Hollander, Patricia A. *Legal Handbook for Education*. Boulder: Westview Press, 1978.

Hudgins, H. C., Jr., and Richard S. Vacca. *Law and Education: Contemporary Issues and Court Decisions*. Charlottesville: Michie, 1979.

Kaplin, William A. *The Law of Higher Education*. San Francisco: Jossey-Bass, 1978.

Korpela, Allen E. "Modern Status of Doctrine of Sovereign Immunity as Applied to Public Schools and Institutions of Higher Learning." Annot. 33 *A.L.R.3d* 703 (1970).

_____. "Tort Liability of Public Schools and Institutions of Higher Learning for Injuries Caused by Acts of Fellow Students." Annot. 36 *A.L.R.3d* 330 (1971).

_____. "Immunity of Private Schools and Institutions of Higher Learning from Liability in Tort." Annot. 38 *A.L.R.3d* 480 (1971).

_____. "Tort Liability of Public Schools and Institutions of Higher Learning for Injuries Resulting from Lack or Insufficiency of Supervision." Annot. 38 *A.L.R.3d* 830 (1971).

_____. "Tort Liability of Private Schools and Institutions of Higher Learning for Negligence of, or Lack of Supervision by, Teachers and Other Employees or Agents." Annot. 38 *A.L.R.3d* 908 (1971).

Ladenson, Alex. "Library Security and the Law," *College and Research Libraries* 38:109 (1977).

McGhehey, M. A., ed. *School Law Update—1977*. Topeka: National Organization of Legal Problems of Education, 1978.

National Organization on Legal Problems of Education. *Current Trends in School Law*. Topeka: National Organization on Legal Problems of Education, 1974.

Nelson, William G. "Control Requisites and Insurance Options Concerning Certain Library Operational Risks," *Journal of Library Administration* 2:1 (1981).

Phay, Robert E. *The Law of Suspension and Expulsion: An Examination of the Substantive Issues in Controlling Student Conduct.* Topeka: National Organization on Legal Problems of Education, 1975.

Piele, Philip K., ed. *The Yearbook of School Law, 1980.* Topeka: National Organization on Legal Problems of Education, 1980.

Prosser, William L. *Handbook of the Law of Torts.* 4th ed. St. Paul: West Publishing, 1971.

Smith, Joel E. "Liability of University, College, or Other School for Failure to Protect Students from Crime." Annot. 1 *A.L.R.4th* 1099 1980).

"Surveillance of Individual Reading Habits: Constitutional Limitations on Disclosure of Library Borrower Lists," *American University Law Review* 30:275 (1981).

Vacca, Richard S., and H. C. Hudgins Jr. *Liability of School Officials and Administrators for Civil Rights Torts.* Charlottesville: Michie, 1982.

Young, D. Parker, ed. *The Yearbook of Higher Education Law, 1977.* Topeka: National Organization on Legal Problems of Education, 1977.

————. *The Yearbook of Higher Education Law, 1978.* Topeka: National Organization on Legal Problems of Education, 1978.

————. *The Yearbook of Higher Education Law, 1979.* Topeka: National Organization on Legal Problems of Education, 1979.

————. *The Yearbook of Higher Education Law, 1980.* Topeka: National Organization on Legal Problems of Education, 1980.

————. *The Yearbook of Higher Education Law, 1981.* Topeka: National Organization on Legal Problems of Education, 1981.

Security

Baron, C. "Open versus Closed Periodical Stacks in a Research Library: How to Study the Question," *North Carolina Libraries* 40:134–140 (Summer 1982).

Brand, Marvine. "Security of Academic Library Buildings," *Library and Archival Security* 3:39–47 (Spring 1980).

Brashear, J. K. "Problem Patrons: The Other Kind of Library Security," *Illinois Librarian* 63:343–351 (April 1981).

Butler, William G. "Asking the Right Questions," *Security Management* 25/3:50 (March 1981). Suggests multistep procedure for selecting the right guard service.

Cronin, M. J. "Workshop Approach to Library Security," *Library and Archival Security* 3:49–56 (Spring 1980).

Daugherty, Robert A., and Others. "Preliminary Report on Book Losses in Libraries: A Pilot Opinion Survey." Washington, D.C.: ERIC, 1977. ED165773. 35p.

Davis, Donna G. "Security Problems in College and University Libraries," *College and Research Libraries* 32:15–22 (Jan. 1971).

Delph, E. W. "Preventing Public Sex in Library Settings," *Library and Archival Security* 3:17–26 (Summer 1980).

DeRose, F. J. "Disruptive Patron," *Library and Archival Security* 3:29–37 (Fall–Winter 1980).

Desmarais, Norman. "Losses in a Theological Library," *College and Research Libraries* 43:393–395 (Sept. 1982).

Dougherty, Richard M. "Preservation and Access: A Collision of Objectives," *Journal of Academic Librarianship* 8:199 (Sept. 1982).

Elser, George C. "Exit Controls and the Statewide Card," *College and Research Libraries* 28:194–196 (May 1967).

Feret, Barbara L. "Point of Sale," *Wilson Library Bulletin* 47:46–47 (Sept. 1972).

Fisher, A. James. *Security for Business and Industry.* Englewood Cliffs, N.J.: Prentice-Hall, 1979.

Gandert, S. R. "Greeks Bearing Gifts and Other Sad Tales," *Library and Archival Security* 4:39–46 (Fall 1982).

————. "Library and Museum Security, Problems in Selected North Eastern Institutions." Thesis, Long Island University, C. W. Post Center, 1980. 230p.

————. "Protecting Your Collection," *Library and Archival Security* 4:nos. 1 and 2 (1982).

Gjettum, Pamela. "Alarm Systems: Library Confronts Criminal Capers," *American Libraries* 9:233–234 (April 1978).

Green, Gion. *Introduction to Security.* 3d ed. Boston: Butterworth, 1981.

Hemphill, Charles F., Jr. *Modern Security Methods.* Englewood Cliffs, N.J.: Prentice-Hall, 1979.

Jenkins, J. H. "Security Procedures," *A B Bookman's Weekly* 69:1224–1239 (15 Feb. 1982).

Kleberg, J. R. "Rx for Library Security," *Library and Archival Security* 4:23–30 (Winter 1982).

Kohl, David F. "High Efficiency Inventorying through Predictive Data," *Journal of Academic Librarianship* 8:82–84 (May 1982).

Lincoln, A. J. "Patterns of Crime and Security in U.S. Public Libraries," *Library and Archival Security* 4:1–11 (Winter 1982).

————, and C. Z. Lincoln. "Impact of Crime in Public Libraries," *Library and Archival Security* 3:125–137 (Fall–Winter 1980).

Lowry, Glenn R. *Application of a Collection Loss Rate Determination Heuristic to the Brigham Young Library.* Provo: Brigham Young University Library, 1979. 17p.

————. "Heuristic Collection Loss Rate Determination Methodology," *Collection Management* 4:73–83 (Spring–Summer 1982).

McCarthy, Joseph, and Esther Perica. "Burglary: A Rising Problem in Library Security," *Unabashed Librarian no.* 37:19–20 (1980).

Miller, Bruce Allen, and Marilyn Sorum. "A Two Stage Sampling Procedure for Estimating the Proportion of Lost Books in a Library," *Journal of Academic Librarianship* 3:74–80 (May 1977).

Monnelly, Margaret. "Library Security in a High School: Is It Feasible?" *Moccasin Telegraph* 20:5–10 (Winter 1978).

Norman, R. V. "Method of Estimating Losses of Checked Out Material," *Nebraska Library Association Quarterly* 9:31–34 (Fall 1980).

Pierce, A. R. *Circulation and Finding System*. Blacksburg: Virginia Polytechnic Institute and State University Library, 1979. 30p.

A Plan to Improve School and Library Environments. Honolulu. Hawaii State Department of Education, 1976. 309p.

Post, Richard S. *Combating Crime against Small Business*. Springfield, Ill.: C. C. Thomas, 1972.

Revill, D. H. "Library Security," *New Library World* 79:75–77 (April 1978).

Riley, William J. "Library Security and the Federal Bureau of Investigation," *College and Research Libraries* 38:104–108 (March 1977).

Roberts, Matt. "Guards, Turnstiles, Electronic Devices, and the Illusion of Security," *College and Research Libraries* 29:270–273 (July 1968).

Robinson, Donald Bruce. "A Survey of the Attitudes towards and Utilization of Security Measures in Selected Academic Libraries." Ph.D. Dissertation, Florida State University, 1976. 137p.

Rovelstad, M. V. "Open Shelves/Closed in Research Libraries," *College and Research Libraries* 37:457–467 (Sept. 1976).

Sager, Don "Protecting the Library after Hours," *Library Journal* 94:3609–3614 (15 Oct. 1969).

Schefrin, Rita A. "The Barriers to and Barriers of Library Security," *Wilson Library Bulletin* 45:870–878 (May 1971).

Schindler, Pat. "Use of Security Guards in Libraries," *Library Security Newsletter* 2:1–6 (Summer 1978).

"Security Problems in Libraries Mount," *Library Journal* 106:1873–1874 (1 Oct. 1981).

Shaughnessy, Thomas W. *Procedures for Inventorying and Replacing Missing Monographs in a Large Research Library*. Houston: University of Houston Libraries, 1981. 10p.

Sheridan, L. W. "People in Libraries as Security Agents," *Library and Archival Security* 3:57–61 (Spring 1980).

Sheridan, Robert N. "Measuring Book Disappearance," *Library Journal* 99:2040–2043 (1 Sept. 1974).

Shill, H. R. "Open Stacks and Library Performance," *College and Research Libraries* 41:220–226 (May 1980).

Simon, Rita James. "Vandalism in a University Library—Who's Responsible?" *Education* 90:39–42 (Sept.–Oct. 1969).

Steeno, David. comp. "The Legal Basis of Authority," *Security Management* 26/5:50 (May 1982). Based on a chapter of a book in progress, *Private Security,* by Charles Schnabolk. Discussion of various kinds of law under which authority may be exercised.

"Technology vs. the Academic Book Thief," *American School and University* 45:25–35 (Oct. 1972).

Trelles, Oscar M. "Protection of Libraries," *Law Library Journal* 98:241–258 (Aug. 1973).

Tuttle, J. A. "Security and Safety: University of Wisconsin, Madison Memorial Library Steps to Solve Problems," *Wisconsin Library Bulletin* 76:135–164 (May/June 1980).

Vasi, John, ed. "Proceedings of the American Library Association Conference Program on Collection Security and Life Safety, San Francisco, June 30, 1981," *Library and Archival Security* 4 #3:9–38 (1982).

Walsh, Robert R. "Theft and Security System Confidentiality," *Library and Archival Security* 2(3/4):24–25 (1978).

Walsh, Timothy J., and Richard J. Healy. *Protection of Assets Manual.* Santa Monica: Merritt, 1982. Five-volume continuing service.

Wayhrauch, Ernest E., and Mary Thurman. "Turnstiles, Checkers and Library Security," *Southeastern Librarian* 18:111–116 (Summer 1968).

Theft and Mutilation

Anson, Brooke. "Foil That Audiovisual Thief!" *Wisconsin Library Bulletin* 74:168+ (July 1978).

Beach, Allyne. "Library Book Theft: A Case Study." Thesis, Ohio State University, 1976. 123p.

Bean, Ruth Anne. "Theft and Mutilation of Books, Magazines and Newspapers," *Library Occurrent* 12:12–15 (Jan.–March 1936).

Cannon, Marvis. "Book Loss: Theft or Apathy," *Indiana Media Journal* 2:23–25 (Summer 1980).

Cook, Colleen. "Serials Inventory: A Case Study," *Serials Librarian* 5:25–30 (Winter 1980).

Edgar, N. L. "Missing (i.e., Mutilated or Stolen) Issue: One Technique for Replacement," *Library Acquisitions* 6 #3:295–304 (1982).

Gandert, S. R. "Fictional Theft and the World of Reality," *Library and Archival Security* 4:47–53 (Fall 1982).

Gouke, M. N., and M. E. Murfin. "Practicing Librarian: Periodical Mutilation, the Insidious Disease," *Library Journal* 105:1795–1797 (15 Sept. 1980).

Griffith, J. W. "Library Thefts: A Problem That Won't Go Away," *American Libraries* 9:224–227 (April 1978).

Hendrick, Clyde, and Marjorie Murfin. "Project Library Ripoff: A Study of Periodical Mutilation in a University Library," *College and Research Libraries* 35:402–411 (November 1974).

Hilterbran, Cathie. "Theft Losses in Ohio School Media Centers," *Ohio Media Spectrum* 33:36–38 (Fall–Winter 1981).

Hoppe, Ronald A., and Edward C. Simmel. "Book Tearing and the Bystander in the University Library," *College and Research Libraries* 30:247–251 (May 1969).

Huttner, Marian A. "Measuring and Reducing Book Losses," *Library Journal* 98:512–513 (15 Feb. 1973).

Kaske, Neal K. *A Report on the Level and Rate of Book Theft from the Main Stacks of the Doe Library at the University of California, Berkeley.* Berkeley: University of California Library, 1977. 70p.

_____. and Donald D. Thompson. *A Report on the Moffitt Undergraduate Library Book Theft Study.* Berkeley: University of California Library, 1975. 20p.

Martin, Ron G. *Current Trends of Periodical Circulation Policies Relative to Attitudes by Librarians towards Causes of Mutilation and Theft in 92 Four-Year Colleges and Universities.* Columbia: University of Missouri, 1972. ED089724. 29p.

Mott, Sharon. "An Edmonton High School Reduces Book Losses," *Canadian Library Journal* 35:45–49 (Feb. 1978).

Murfin, Marjorie E., and Clyde Hendrick. "Rip-offs Tell Their Story: Interviews with Mutilators in a University Library," *Journal of Academic Librarianship* 1:8–12 (May 1975).

Niland, Powell, and William H. Kurth. "Estimating Lost Volumes in a University Library Collection," *College and Research Libraries* 27:132 (March 1976).

Paris, Janelle A. "School Library Theft," *Library and Archival Security* 3:29–38 (Spring 1980).

Pinzelik, Barbara. "Monitoring Book Losses in a Large Academic Library: Four Methods." Washington, D.C.: ERIC, 1979. ED203852. 18p.

Reneker, Maxine H. "A Study of Book Thefts in Academic Libraries." Ph.D. dissertation, University of Chicago, 1970. 262p.

Rostenberg, L. and M. B. Caveat Stern. "Book Thief," *Library and Archival Security* 4:13–21 (Winter 1982).

Sleep, Esther L. "Periodical Vandalism: A Chronic Condition?" *Canadian Library Journal* 39:39–42 (Feb. 1982).

"Theft Guidelines Now ABAA Policy," *A B Bookman's Weekly* 64:2252 (8 Oct. 1979).

Van Oosbree, Charlyne. "Book 'em! or, Case of the Missing Books," *Show-Me Libraries* 31:37–40 (May 1980).

Vinnes, Norman. "A Search for Meaning in Book Thefts," *School Library* 18:25–27 (Spring 1969).

Weiss, Dana. "Book Theft and Book Mutilation in a Large Urban University," *College and Research Libraries* 42:341–347 (July 1981).

CONTRIBUTORS

BARBARA BINTLIFF
is Reference Librarian–Technical Services Coordinator, University of Denver Law Library, Denver, Colorado. She is actively engaged in institutes, workshops, and committee activities in library associations and the Colorado Bar Association. As a practicing librarian, Dr. Bintliff deals with security measures on a daily basis. Her latest publication is "Statutes of Limitations for Court Actions in Colorado," 12 *Colorado Lawyer* 895 (1983).

MARVINE BRAND,
retired, who resides at Lake Sam Rayburn, Jasper, Texas, is a former Librarian and Associate Professor at the University of Houston–University Park, Houston, Texas. A number of related positions, including Assistant to the Director of Libraries and Administrative Assistant, were a catalyst for her involvement in and continuing concern for library security. She is the author of "Security of Academic Library Buildings," which appeared in *Library and Archival Security* 3, 39 (1980).

AL (ALFRED) COCO
is Professor of Law and Librarianship and Law Librarian, University of Denver College of Law, Denver, Colorado. Dr. Coco is also Director of the Master of Law Librarianship Program at the University of Denver College of Law and Graduate School of Librarianship and Information Management. He is a consultant for law firms, law libraries, and schools

of law throughout the United States. He could easily add the subject of library security to his growing list of consulting specialties. Of his many publications, the most recent is *Finding the Law: A Workbook on Legal Research for Laypersons* (Washington, D.C.: Government Printing Office, 1982).

WILBUR B. CRIMMIN

retired as Chief Librarian, Hartford (Connecticut) Public Library, in spring of 1984. His interest in security dates from a Staff Association Welfare Committee chairmanship in the 1960s to recent administrative and staff reviews of security in the Hartford Public Library. He is active in the Connecticut Library Association and the American Library Association.

JANELLE A. PARIS

is an Associate Professor, School of Library Science, Sam Houston State University, Huntsville, Texas. Dr. Paris is a former school librarian and has sponsored a workshop dealing specifically with the maintenance and control of library materials. She is presently conducting surveys in Texas on school library fines and school library theft, and is the author of "School Library Theft," *Library and Archival Security* 3, 29 (1980).

THOMAS W. SHAUGHNESSY

is Director of Libraries, University of Missouri–Columbia, Missouri. He has implemented security systems and improved procedures in libraries with which he has been associated. Four of these libraries are Rutgers–Newark Campus, University of Houston, University of Missouri, and Pennsylvania State Library. Dr. Shaughnessy earlier served on the faculty of library schools at the University of Southern California and at Rutgers. He is the author of numerous articles and is currently researching the question of personal security perceptions of library users.

W. WALTER WICKER

is Director of Libraries and Interim Dean of Professional Education at the University of Houston–Clear Lake, Houston, Texas. Dr. Wicker teaches a class in Library Administration, which includes a unit on library security, and is a member of a Texas Council of State University Libraries committee, dealing with preservation of library resources and natural disasters. He has had substantial experience in consulting, planning, and administering libraries, media centers, and regional library systems, and has served on accreditation visiting teams of the Southern Association of Colleges and Schools.